MAKE YOUR OWN LIQUEURS

MAKE YOUR OWN
LIQUEURS

JEAN DICKSON

DESIGN AND ILLUSTRATIONS
BENNIE KRÜGER

δelος

CAPE TOWN

The publishers would like to thank the following people for their contribution to the photographic session with regard to this book:

Deon and Marlene van der Westhuizen
Danie en Albie Esterhuyse
Liesje Smith
David Bell
Arie Roos

Delos, 40 Heerengracht, Cape Town

All rights reserved.
No part of this book may be reproduced or transmitted in any form or by any means, electronic or mechanical, including photocopying, recording or by any information and retrieval system, without permission in writing from the publisher.

© 1991 Delos

Photography by Anton de Beer
Styling by Nanette van Rooyen
Illustrations by Bennie Krüger
Book design by Bennie Krüger
Cover design by Etienne van Duyker

Set in 11/12 pt Bembo
Set by Hirt & Carter (Edms) Bpk
Printed and bound by Toppan Company (H.K.) Ltd, Hong Kong

ISBN 1-86826-138-7

CONTENTS

9
BASIC METHOD
TO MAKE LIQUEUR

10
VARIETY AND AVAILABILITY
OF FRUIT, LEAVES AND NUTS

13
HERBS, SPICES
AND GARDEN PLANTS

15
EQUIPMENT

16
STERILISATION AND BOTTLING

18
FRUIT LIQUEUR WITH AN
ALCOHOL AND SUGAR BASE

53
FRUIT CREAM AND
INSTANT LIQUEUR

INTRODUCTION

Whether you have a sweet tooth or whether you prefer a more bitter taste, there is a liqueur to suit every palate.

Liqueurs have a long history and many secret recipes were buried in the monasteries together with the old monks. Not all was lost though, and in this collection of recipes for liqueurs you will find a treasure of sweet, home-made potions to crown every meal.

I trust that every person who tries these recipes will derive great enjoyment from them.

BASIC METHOD TO MAKE LIQUEUR

The basic principles of making fruit liqueur are very simple:

★ Weigh the clean, peeled and stoned fruit, the nuts and the sugar.
★ Place the fruit and spices or herbs in a clean, dry glass or earthenware container with a tight-fitting lid. Add the alcohol, mix well and close. Leave to stand in a warm, sunny spot indoors. Shake regularly to spread the flavour of the ingredients.
★ First pour the fruit alcohol mixture through a clean sieve and then through a single layer or various layers of the cheesecloth pegged firmly to the edges of the glass bowl. The aim of this procedure is to clarify the liqueur.
★ Pour the sugar, water or wine into the heavy-bottomed pot and heat at a low temperature while stirring. Then bring to boiling point and boil until the syrup has the right consistency. Remove from the stove.
★ Leave the syrup to cool. Add the flavoured alcohol to the cold syrup. Pour the liqueur into the sterilised bottles, cork, seal and stick on the marked etiquette. Store and leave to mature according to the instructions - this improves the flavour.

VARIETY AND AVAILABILITY OF FRUIT, LEAVES AND NUTS

With the abundance of fruit available in the different seasons, you can pick and choose what to use for a liqueur. Below is an indication of the seasons during which the fruit, leaves and nuts used in these recipes are available:

Apples
Throughout the year because of cold storage.

Apricots
December to February.

Bananas
November to January.

Blackberries
December to February.

Cherries
November to January.

Figs
September to March.

Granadillas
January to November.

Guavas
May to November.

Lemons
Throughout the year.

Litchis
December to February.

Loquats
September to October.

Marulas
March to April.

Mulberries
October to November.

Naartjies
May to November.

Oranges
March to October.

Papino's
May to December.

Peaches
November to March.

Pears
January to November.

Pineapples
Throughout the year.

Plums
November to February.

Pomegranates
January to February.

Rose Petals
September to April.

Strawberries
Transvaal:
August to October.

Western Cape:
October to December.

Sweet Melon
November to February.

Walnuts
December.

HERBS, SPICES AND GARDEN PLANTS

Angelica (archangel)

A perennial herb with a thick hollow stem that grows up to 2,5 m high, large leaves and small yellow flowers; familiar as the green sugared pieces that are used to decorate cakes; available from herbal gardeners.

Aniseed

A perennial plant that grows about 30 cm high; available from herbal gardeners; the dried seed has a very strong aroma and is available from super markets and spice merchants.

Caraway

The seed is generally used for baking; available from supermarkets and spice merchants.

Cardamom

The seeds look like dried orange pips; available from supermarkets and spice merchants.

Carnations

A perennial plant that flowers from spring to early summer and bears deep purple flowers that smell like cloves; available from nurseries.

Cinnamon & Cassia

Cinnamon and cassia are sometimes confused with one another because they are both derived from the bark of young trees; cinnamon is sweet with a subtle aroma and is used in sweet dishes, whereas cassia is more suited to meat and savoury dishes; available from supermarkets and spice merchants.

Coriander

A perennial plant that grows up to 60 cm high and has serrated leaves and seed with a pleasant aroma; the plants are available from herbal gardeners and the seed from supermarkets and spice merchants.

Cumin

The seed has an over-powering aroma and should be used sparingly; popular in Indian cooking; available from supermarkets, spice merchants and Eastern shops.

Elder

A shrub with creamy white flowers that smell like honey (which can be dipped in a batter, deep-fried and served with tea) and bunches of black berries; available from nurseries.

Fenugreek

Dried seed that is used to grow sprouts; very popular in Indian cooking; available from spice merchants.

Fennel

A perennial plant with feathery bronze or green leaves and yellow-green flowers; the leaves and seed have a sweet aniseed flavour; the dried seed is available from supermarkets.

Geraniums

A member of the pelargonium family; those with a fruity aroma are ideal for liqueurs; available from herbal gardeners.

Hyssop

A perennial evergreen plant with strongly aromatic leaves; grown from seed or cuttings; available from herbal gardeners.

Mace

The dried shell around nutmeg; available from spice merchants.

Rosemary

A perennial plant; the leaves have a strong aroma and should be used sparingly; available from nurseries and herbal gardeners.

Verbena

A perennial plant with small white or purple flowers; the bruised leaf has a sharp lemon aroma; available from herbal gardeners.

Violets

A perennial plant with pleasantly scented pink, violet blue or white flowers in winter; available from nurseries.

EQUIPMENT

Using the right equipment facilitates making liqueurs.

Cheesecloth
A single layer or various layers of fine cheesecloth are used to strain the mixtures for clear liqueurs.

Corks
Only new corks which are available from manufacturers (look in the Yellow Pages for suppliers of winery equipment), should be used.

Etiquettes
These are used to write down the name and date of preparation of the liqueurs and are then stuck on the containers.

Flasks, bottles and earthenware containers
Earthenware containers with corks are best. Clean jam jars with screw lids or salad dressing, chutney or tomato sauce bottles (catering size) are used to let fruit alcohol mixtures stand in. The containers should have wide necks so that the ingredients can be spooned in easily. Sterilised liquor bottles are used to keep the liqueurs in.

Flour sieve
This is used to pour fruit alcohol mixtures through to obtain clear liqueurs.

Funnel
This is used to pour the liqueers into bottles and flasks.

Glass bowl
This is used to strain fruit alchol mixtures into.

Pegs
These are used to peg the cheesecloth, stretched firmly over the bowl, to the edges.

Pliers
These are used to lift the sterilised bottles and flasks from the boiling water.

Pots
A medium heavy-bottomed pot 18,5 cm in diameter and approximately 11 cm high is used to prepare the liqueurs in. A deep pot is used to sterilise the bottles and flasks in.

Pot rack
The type that is sold with pressure cookers is preferable. It is placed inside the deep pot and is used to hold the containers when they are being sterilised.

Scale
This is used to weigh the fruit and sugar.

Sealing or candle wax
This is used to seal the corks and necks of the bottles and flasks.

Wooden spoon
Using a wooden spoon with a long handle will prevent the sugar syrup from burning your hands.

STERILISATION AND BOTTLING

To make it even easier for the beginner, only one sterilisation method is used:
* Wash the glass or earthenware containers in soap water and rinse well with clean water.
* Place the pot rack on the bottom of the deep pot.
* Fill the containers with warm water and place on the pot rack in the pot. Fill the pot with hot water and boil for 10 minutes.
* Remove the sterilised containers with the pliers when required.

Use the following method to bottle the liqueurs:
* Boil the corks for 10 minutes to soften them.
* Fill the sterilised bottles and flasks by pouring the liqueurs into them through the funnel.
* Cork the bottles or flasks tightly and seal with the sealing or candle wax by covering both the corks and the bottle necks.
* Write the name and date of preparation of the liqueurs on the etiquettes and stick them on the filled bottles.
* Store the liqueurs according to the instructions for each recipe.

FRUIT LIQUEUR WITH AN ALCOHOL AND SUGAR BASE

ANGELICA LIQUEUR

Angelica is familiar as the green sugared pieces that are used to decorate cakes.

• **INGREDIENTS** •

100 g fresh angelica
1 piece of mace
4 cm piece of cassia
4 cloves
750 ml brandy
600 g (750 ml) sugar
750 ml water

• **METHOD** •

Cut the stem of the angelica into pieces.

Place the angelica, mace, cassia and cloves in a clean glass or earthenware container with a tight-fitting lid. Pour in the brandy and close. Leave to stand for a month in a warm spot. Shake every morning and evening.

Strain the mixture through cheesecloth, repeating if it is not clear. Set aside.

Mix the sugar and water in a heavy-bottomed pot, heat over a very low temperature and stir until the sugar has melted. Bring to boiling point and boil for 17 minutes. Remove the syrup from the stove and leave to cool. Add the flavoured brandy to the cold syrup.

Pour the liqueur into the dry, sterilised bottles, cork, seal and mark. Store for at least two months before using, although it tastes best after a year.

• **CONTAINERS** •

Sterilise 2 x 750 ml bottles. Makes 1,4 ℓ.

ANISEED LIQUEUR

Pure heaven! The aniseed flavour of this clear honey-brown liqueur lingers in the mouth.

• INGREDIENTS •

40 g (125 ml) aniseed
750 ml brandy
500 g (625 ml) sugar
750 ml water

• METHOD •

Place the aniseed in a clean jam jar with a screw lid and add the brandy. Close the jar tightly and shake. Leave to stand for a fortnight in a warm spot. Shake well regularly.

Strain the mixture through two layers of cheesecloth. Set aside.

Mix the sugar and water in a heavy-bottomed pot over a low temperature and stir until the sugar has melted. Bring to boiling point and boil for 17 minutes. Remove the syrup from the stove and leave to cool. Add the flavoured brandy to the cold syrup and mix.

Pour the liqueur into the dry, sterilised bottles, cork, seal and mark. Store for at least a month before use.

• CONTAINERS •

Sterilise 1ℓ bottle.
Makes 1,1 ℓ.

APPLE AND FENNEL LIQUEUR

This unusual combination guarantees a surprising taste sensation, the fennel providing a distinctive aniseed flavour. The lace-like leaves, the seeds and the bulbs can be used.

• INGREDIENTS •

500 g apples
1 sprig of fennel
2 cardamom seeds
400 g (500 ml) sugar
750 ml cider
500 ml gin

• METHOD •

Halve, seed and cut the apples into pieces.

Place the apple, fennel, cardamom and sugar in a pot and add the cider. Bring slowly to boiling point and stir until the sugar has melted. Remove the syrup from the stove and leave to cool. Stir the gin into the cold syrup.

Pour the mixture into a glass or earthenware container, close tightly and leave to stand for a week. Shake every morning and evening.

Strain the mixture through cheesecloth, repeating if necessary.

Pour the liqueur into the dry, sterilised bottles, cork, seal and mark. Store for a month before use.

• CONTAINERS •

Sterilise 1ℓ + 250 ml bottles.
Makes 1,25 ℓ

APPLE LIQUEUR

Like any other apple drink, this liqueur will appeal to everyone.

• **INGREDIENTS** •

700 g apples
4 cm piece of cassia
2 cardamom seeds
400 g (500 ml) sugar
750 ml cider
500 ml vodka

• **METHOD** •

Halve, seed and cut the apples into pieces.

Place the apple, cassia, cardamom, sugar and cider in a pot. Bring slowly to boiling point. Stir constantly until the sugar has melted. Remove the syrup from the stove and leave to cool. Add the vodka to the cold syrup.

Pour the mixture into a glass or earthenware container and close. Leave to stand for a week. Shake every morning and evening.

Strain the mixture through two layers of cheesecloth.

Pour the liqueur into the dry, sterilised bottles, cork, seal and mark. Store for a month before use.

• **CONTAINERS** •

Sterilise 1ℓ + 250 ml bottles. Makes 1,25 ℓ.

APRICOT LIQUEUR (1)

This yellow fruit with the pale blush is a good choice for a liqueur.

• **CONTAINERS** •

14 ripe apricots
750 ml brandy
5 ml allspice (pimento)
300 g (375 ml) sugar

• **METHOD** •

Halve the apricots (retain the stones) and cut into pieces or pulp in a food processor. Crack the stones with a heavy rolling pin, remove the kernels and pull off the skin.

Place all the ingredients in a wide-necked glass flask, close tightly and shake well. Leave to stand for a month.

Pour the mixture first through a clean sieve and then strain through three layers of cheesecloth.

Pour the liqueur into the dry, sterilised bottles, cork, seal and mark. Store for a month before use.

• **INGREDIENTS** •

Sterilise 1 x 750 ml bottle. Makes 800 ml.

APRICOT LIQUEUR (2)

It is a good idea to double this recipe because a bottle of apricot liqueur makes a sought-after Christmas or birthday present.

• INGREDIENTS •

500 g fresh apricots
5 ml whole allspice
500 g (625 ml) sugar
750 ml dry white wine
400 ml gin
50 ml white rum

• METHOD •

Halve the apricots (retain the stones). Crack the stones with a heavy rolling pin, remove the kernels and pull off the skin.

Place the apricots, allspice, sugar and wine in an enamel pot. Heat over a low temperature and stir until the sugar has melted. Remove the syrup from the stove and leave to cool. Add the apricot kernels, gin and rum.

Pour the mixture into a glass flask with a lid, close tightly and leave to stand for a fortnight.

Strain the mixture through cheesecloth.

Pour the liqueur into the dry, sterilised bottles, cork, seal and mark. Store for a month before use.

• CONTAINERS •

Sterilise 1 ℓ bottle.
Makes 1,1 ℓ.

BANANA LIQUEUR

This all-round fruit makes a yellow liqueur.

• INGREDIENTS •

7 medium, ripe bananas
750 ml brandy
400 g (500 ml) sugar
250 ml water

• METHOD •

Peel and slice the bananas thinly.

Place the banana in a clean glass or earthenware container with a tightly-fitting lid. Add the brandy, close tightly and leave to stand for five weeks in a warm spot. Shake regularly.

Pour the mixture first through a clean, dry sieve and then strain through four layers of cheesecloth. Set aside. Mix the sugar and water in a heavy-bottomed pot and stir until the sugar has melted. Bring to boiling point and boil for 12 minutes. Remove the syrup from the stove and leave to cool. Add the flavoured brandy to the cold syrup.

Pour the liqueur into the dry, sterilised bottles, cork, seal and mark. Store for a month before use.

• CONTAINERS •

Sterilise 1 ℓ bottle.
Makes 900 ml.

BLACKBERRY LIQUEUR (1)

If you are familiar with blackberries, you will recognise the flavour of this red-purple liqueur with the first sip.

• INGREDIENTS •

500 g (625 ml) sugar
750 ml dry white wine
500 g fresh blackberries
750 ml gin

• METHOD •

Place the sugar and wine in a pot and stir over a low temperature until the sugar has melted. Add the blackberries and bring to the boil. Remove the syrup from the stove, leave to cool and add the gin.

Pour the mixture into a clean, dry glass or earthenware container with a tightly-fitting lid. Close and leave to stand for a month in a warm spot. Shake at least twice a day.

Strain the mixture through three layers of cheesecloth.

Pour the liqueur into the dry, sterilised bottle, cork, seal and mark. Store for at least a week before use.

• CONTAINERS •

Sterilise 1 ℓ + 750 ml bottles.
Makes 1,7 ℓ.

Photograph on p 29

BLACKBERRY LIQUEUR (2)

Because the witblits, which forms the base of this liqueur, has an almost neutral flavour, the taste of the fresh blackberries comes through strongly. Characteristic of this liqueur is its deep red-purple colour.

• INGREDIENTS •

500 g fresh blackberries
750 ml witblits
600 g (750 ml) sugar
750 ml water

• METHOD •

Place the blackberries in a clean, dry glass or earthenware container with a tightly-fitting lid. Add the witblits and close. Leave to stand for a month in a warm spot. Shake every morning and evening.

Place the sugar and water in a heavy-bottomed pot. (It is advisable to stir the sugar and water so that the sugar melts before it is heated.) Bring the mixture to the boil and boil for 17 minutes. Remove the syrup from the stove and leave to cool.

Pour the mixture through a sieve and strain through three layers of cheesecloth. Add the cold syrup.

Pour the liqueur into the dry, sterilised bottle, cork, seal and mark. Store for at least a fortnight before use.

• CONTAINERS •

Sterilise 1 ℓ bottle.
Makes 1,15 ℓ.

BLUEBERRY LIQUEUR

Blueberries have an interesting, slightly sour flavour that improves with cooking.

• INGREDIENTS •

500 g blueberries
6 ml allspice
500 g (625 ml) sugar
750 ml dry white wine
500 ml vodka

• METHOD •

Remove the stems from the blueberries.

Place the blueberries, allspice and sugar in a pot. Add the wine. Bring to boiling point and stir until the sugar has melted. Remove the syrup from the stove and leave to cool. Add the vodka to the cold syrup.

Pour the mixture into a clean, dry glass or earthenware container and close tightly. Leave to stand for 10 days in a warm spot. Shake every morning and evening.

Strain the mixture through cheesecloth, squeezing as much of the liqueur from the blueberries as possible.

Pour the liqueur into the dry, sterilised bottles, cork, seal and mark. Store for at least a month before use.

• CONTAINERS •

Sterilise 2 x 750 ml bottles.
Makes 1,5 ℓ.

CARNATION LIQUEUR

Have you ever imagined a scent of cloves when smelling carnations? - believe it next time you smell a purple or wine-red carnation!

• INGREDIENTS •

500 ml purple or wine-red carnation petals smelling strongly of cloves
1 sprig of verbena or a 5 cm piece of lemon peel
10 cloves
1 ℓ brandy
600 g (750 ml) sugar
750 ml water

• METHOD •

Remove the white parts of the carnation petals.

Place the carnation petals, verbena or lemon peel and cloves in a wide-necked glass flask. Add the brandy. Close the flask tightly and shake. Leave to stand for three weeks in a warm spot. Shake every morning and evening.

Strain the mixture through cheesecloth, repeating if necessary. Set aside.

Mix the sugar and water in a heavy-bottomed pot over a low temperature until the sugar has melted. Bring to boiling point and boil for 17 minutes. Remove the syrup from the stove and leave to cool. Stir the flavoured brandy into the cold syrup.

Pour the liqueur into the dry, sterilised bottles, cork, seal and mark. Store for at least a month before use.

• CONTAINERS •

Sterilise 1ℓ + 250 ml bottles.
Makes 1,25 ℓ.

CHERRY LIQUEUR

Red cherries are slightly sour, so rather use black cherries, which are sweeter and make an attractive dark liqueur.

• **INGREDIENTS** •

500 g fresh cherries
750 ml brandy
600 g (750 ml) sugar
750 ml water

• **METHOD** •

Remove the stems from the cherries, halve and stone. Mash the cherries with a potato masher.

Place the cherries in a wide-necked glass container with a lid. Add the brandy, close tightly and leave to stand for three weeks in a warm spot. Shake every morning and evening.

Strain the mixture through cheesecloth and repeat if necessary. Set aside.

Mix the sugar and water in a heavy-bottomed pot and stir over a very low temperature until the sugar has melted. Bring to boiling point and boil for 17 minutes. Remove the syrup from the stove and leave to cool. Add the flavoured brandy to the cold syrup.

Pour the liqueur into the dry, sterilised bottles, cork, seal and mark. Store for at least a month before use.

• **CONTAINERS** •

Sterilise 1 ℓ + 250 ml bottles. Makes 1,15 ℓ.

Photograph on p 12

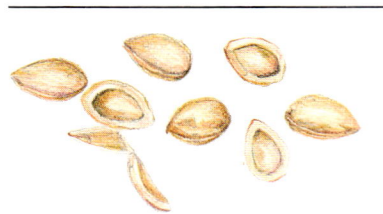

CHERRY STONE LIQUEUR

Economy at its best because even the stones are used in the liqueur!

• **INGREDIENTS** •

stones of 500 g fresh cherries
300 g (375 ml) sugar
750 ml brandy

• **METHOD** •

Wash and dry the stones well. Break the stones and kernels with a heavy rolling pin.

Place the broken stones, kernels and sugar in a clean, dry glass or earthenware container with a lid. Add the brandy, close the container tightly and leave to stand for a month in a warm spot. Shake at least twice a day.

Strain the mixture through cheesecloth. Pour the liqueur into the dry, sterilised bottles, cork, seal and mark. Store for at least a month before use.

• **CONTAINERS** •

Sterilise 1 x 750 ml bottle. Makes 850 ml.

CITRUS LIQUEUR

Only the peel of oranges, lemons and naartjies is used in this liqueur.

• **INGREDIENTS** •

3 oranges
3 lemons
1 naartjie
5 cloves
750 ml brandy
300 g (375 ml) sugar
375 ml water

• **METHOD** •

Peel the oranges and lemons with a vegetable peeler. Peel the naartjie and scrape the pith from the peel with a teaspoon.

Place the peel and cloves in a dry glass container with a lid. Add the brandy, close tightly and leave to stand for a fortnight in a warm spot. Shake every morning and evening.

Strain the mixture through two layers of cheesecloth. Set aside.

Mix the sugar and water in a heavy-bottomed pot and stir until the sugar has melted. Bring to boiling point and boil for 15 minutes. Remove the syrup from the stove and leave to cool. Add the flavoured brandy to the cold syrup.

Pour the liqueur into the dry, sterilised bottles, cork, seal and mark. Store for a month before use.

• **CONTAINERS** •

Sterilise 1ℓ bottle.
Makes 900 ml.

COFFEE BEAN LIQUEUR

A bonus for coffee lovers!

• **INGREDIENTS** •

10 mocha coffee beans
750 ml white rum
300 g (375 ml) sugar

• **METHOD** •

Place the coffee beans in a clean, dry glass or earthenware container with a lid. Add the rum, close tightly and leave to stand for two months in a warm spot. Shake regularly.

Add the sugar to the mixture and stir well until the sugar has melted. Strain the mixture through cheesecloth.

Pour the liqueur into the dry, sterilised bottles, cork, seal and mark. Store for at least a month before use.

• **CONTAINERS** •

Sterilise 1 x 750 ml bottle.
Makes 850 ml.

COFFEE LIQUEUR

A must to round off a convivial get-together.

• INGREDIENTS •

30 ml instant coffee powder
20 ml boiling water
30 ml rum
600 ml brandy
1 vanilla pod
600 g (750 ml) sugar
750 ml water

• METHOD •

Mix the instant coffee powder with the boiling water. Pour the mixed coffee, rum, brandy and vanilla pod into a glass flask. Close tightly and leave to stand for a fortnight in a warm spot. Shake every morning and evening.

Mix the sugar and water in a heavy-bottomed pot and stir until the sugar has melted. Bring to boiling point and boil for 17 minutes. Remove the syrup from the stove and leave to cool. Remove the vanilla pod. Add the flavoured brandy to the cold syrup.

Pour the liqueur into the dry, sterilised bottle, cork, seal and mark. Store for at least six months before use.

• CONTAINERS •

Sterilise 1 ℓ bottle.
Makes 1,05 ℓ.

ELDER LIQUEUR

The berries and honey-scented flowers of the elder are used in this liqueur.

• INGREDIENTS •

600 g elder berries
3 elder flowers
30 ml grated orange peel (without the pith)
30 ml grated lemon peel (without the pith)
300 ml late harvest wine
750 ml cane spirit
500 g (625 ml) sugar
650 ml water

• METHOD •

Remove the stems from the berries. Place the berries, flowers and peel in a heavy-bottomed pot. Add the wine, bring slowly to the boil and boil until the berries are soft. Remove from the stove and leave to cool.

Place the berries in a clean glass container with a lid. Add the cane, close tightly and leave to stand for a fortnight in a warm spot. Shake every morning and evening.

Pour the mixture first through a clean sieve and then strain through two layers of cheesecloth, repeating if necessary. Set aside.

Mix the sugar and water in a heavy-bottomed pot and stir over a low temperature until the sugar has melted. Bring to the boil and boil for 15 minutes. Remove the syrup from the stove and leave to cool. Add the flavoured cane to the cold syrup.

Pour the liqueur into the dry, sterilised bottles, cork, seal and mark. Store for a month before use.

• CONTAINERS •

Sterilise 2 x 750 ml bottles.
Makes 1,45 ℓ.

FIG LEAF LIQUEUR

A light green liqueur that tastes like green fig jam.

• INGREDIENTS •

500g (625 ml) sugar
750 ml water
12 fig leaves
750 ml gin

• METHOD •

Mix the sugar and water in a saucepan with a heavy bottom with a wooden spoon until the sugar has dissolved. Wash the fig leaves and add them to the sugar and water mixture. Heat to boiling point and cook for 20 minutes. Remove the mixture from the stove, remove fig leaves and let the syrup cool. Add the gin to the cold syrup.

Pour the liqueur into the dry, sterilized bottles, cork, seal and mark. Let stand for one month before using.

• CONTAINERS •

Sterilize 1 x 750 ml and 1 x 500 ml bottles. Makes 1,15 litres.

Photograph opposite p 9

GRANADILLA LIQUEUR

For this recipe, use the purple variety of granadilla - it has a stronger flavour.

• INGREDIENTS •

25 granadillas
15 ml grated lemon peel
750 ml vodka
600 g (750 ml) sugar
750 ml water

• METHOD •

Halve the granadillas and remove the pulp.

Place the pulp and peel in a clean, dry glass flask with a tightly-fitting lid. Add the vodka, close and leave to stand for a month at room temperature. Shake daily.

Strain the mixture through four layers of cheesecloth. Set aside.

Mix the sugar and water in a heavy-bottomed pot and heat over a low temperature until the sugar has melted. Bring to the boil and boil for 17 minutes. Remove the syrup from the stove and leave to cool. Add the flavoured vodka to the cold syrup and stir well.

Pour the liqueur into the dry, sterilised bottles, cork, seal and mark. Store for at least a week before use.

• CONTAINERS •

Sterilise 1 ℓ bottle. Makes 1,15 ℓ.

GRAPEFRUIT LIQUEUR

This is a liqueur with a deliciously refreshing taste. Use the grapefruit with the pink peel and flesh (rose) - this variety is sweeter and, in addition, seedless. The colour is drawn out by the gin - hence the rose colour of the liqueur.

• INGREDIENTS •

3 grapefruit
500 g (625 ml) sugar
1 sprig of fresh mint
1 ℓ gin

• METHOD •

Peel the grapefruit very thinly with a vegetable peeler (do not peel the pith). Cut the peel into pieces. Halve the grapefruit and squeeze out the juice.

Mix the peel, juice, sugar and mint and pour into a glass or earthenware container with a lid. Add the gin and close tightly. Leave to stand for eight weeks in a warm spot. Shake every morning and evening.

Strain the mixture through cheesecloth. Pour the liqueur into the dry, sterilised bottles, cork, seal and mark. Store for a month before use.

• CONTAINERS •

Sterilise 1 ℓ + 750 ml bottles. Makes 1,6 ℓ.

GREEN WALNUT LIQUEUR

Green walnuts look like small green pears. Wear gloves when you chop the walnuts, otherwise your hands will be stained black. The liqueur has a nutty flavour and the colour is a surprise!

• INGREDIENTS •

15 green walnuts
15 g stick cinnamon
7 g cloves
750 ml schnapps
600 g (750 ml) sugar
800 ml water

• METHOD •

Chop up the walnuts. Place the walnuts, cinnamon and cloves in a clean, dry glass container with a tightly-fitting lid. Add the schnapps, close and leave to stand for three weeks in a warm spot. Shake every morning and evening.

Pour the mixture first through a clean, dry sieve and then strain through two layers of cheesecloth. Set aside.

Mix the sugar and water in a heavy-bottomed pot and stir until the sugar has melted. Bring to the boil and boil for 18 minutes. Remove the syrup from the stove and leave to cool. Add the flavoured schnapps to the cold syrup.

Pour the liqueur into the dry, sterilised bottles, cork, seal and mark. Store for at least six months before use.

• CONTAINERS •

Sterilise 1 ℓ bottle. Makes 1,15 ℓ.

GUAVA LIQUEUR

Guavas, a tropical fruit with a strong flavour, are ideal for liqueurs.

• INGREDIENTS •

500 g guavas
4 cloves
1 piece of stick cinnamon
750 ml cane spirit
500 g sugar
600 ml water

• METHOD •

Peel the guavas and cut into small pieces.

Place the guava, cloves and cinnamon in a clean, dry glass or earthenware container with a lid. Add the cane, close tightly and shake well. Leave to stand for a fortnight in a warm spot. Shake at least twice a day.

Pour the mixture first through a clean, dry sieve and then strain through two layers of cheesecloth. Set aside.

Mix the sugar and water in a heavy-bottomed pot and stir until the sugar has melted. Bring to the boil and boil for 18 minutes. Remove the syrup from the stove and leave to cool. Add the flavoured cane to the cold syrup.

Pour the liqueur into the dry, sterilised bottle, cork, seal and mark. Store for a month before use.

• CONTAINERS •

Sterilise 1 ℓ bottle. Makes 1,15 ℓ.

HYSSOP LIQUEUR

If this pleasantly-scented plant does not yet grow in your herb garden, now is the time to plant it. The leaves and the flowers are said to have been two of the secret ingredients with which the monks of old flavoured their liqueurs!

• INGREDIENTS •

5 oranges
2 lemons
4 x 4 cm sprigs of hyssop
4 hyssop flowers
5 cloves
4 cm piece of cassia
1 ℓ brandy
750 g (640 ml) sugar
800 ml water

• METHOD •

Peel the oranges and lemons very thinly with a vegetable peeler (do not peel the pith). Bruise the hyssop sprigs.

Place the peel, hyssop sprigs and flowers, cloves and cassia in a wide-necked glass flask with a lid. Add the brandy, close tightly and leave to stand for a fortnight in a warm spot. Shake every morning and evening.

Pour the mixture first through a clean sieve and then strain through cheesecloth, repeating if necessary. Set aside.

Mix the sugar and water in a heavy-bottomed pot and stir over a very low temperature until the sugar has melted. Bring to boiling point and boil for 17 minutes. Remove the syrup from the stove and leave to cool. Add the flavoured brandy to the cold syrup.

Pour the liqueur into the dry, sterilised bottles, cork, seal and mark. Store for at least a month before use.

• CONTAINERS •

Sterilise 1 ℓ + 750 ml bottles.

KÜMMEL LIQUEUR

A liqueur made from caraway seed, cumin and fennel seed.

• INGREDIENTS •

12 g caraway seed
12 g cumin
12 g fennel seed
4 cm piece of stick cinnamon
1 ℓ brandy
500 g (625 ml) sugar
650 ml water

• METHOD •

Bruise the caraway seed, cumin and fennel seed.
   Place the seeds and cinnamon in a clean, dry glass container with a tightly-fitting lid. Add the brandy, close and leave to stand for a fortnight in a warm spot. Shake every morning and evening.
   Strain the mixture through cheesecloth and repeat if necessary. Set aside.
   Mix the sugar and water in a heavy-bottomed pot and stir over a very low temperature until the sugar has melted. Bring to boiling point and boil for 15 minutes. Remove the syrup from the stove and leave to cool. Add the flavoured brandy to the cold syrup and mix well.
   Pour the liqueur into the dry, sterilised bottles, cork, seal and mark. Store for at least a month before use.

• CONTAINERS •

Sterilise 2 x 750 ml bottles.
Makes 1,45 ℓ.

LEMON LIQUEUR

Lemons are freely available but unfortunately too sour to eat. You can, however, use the peel for this liqueur, and freeze the juice.

• INGREDIENTS •

5 lemons
2 mint leaves
3 lemon-scented geranium leaves
750 ml cane spirit
600 g (750 ml) sugar
750 ml water

• METHOD •

Peel the lemons very thinly with a vegetable peeler.
   Place the peel, mint and geranium leaves in a wide-necked glass flask with a screw lid. Add the cane, close and leave to stand for a fortnight in a warm spot. Shake every morning and evening.
   Strain the mixture through cheesecloth. Set aside.
   Mix the sugar and water in a heavy-bottomed pot and stir until the sugar has melted. Bring to the boil and boil for 17 minutes. Remove the syrup from the stove and leave to cool. Add the flavoured cane to the cold syrup.
   Pour the liqueur into the dry, sterilised bottles, cork, seal and mark. Store for a fortnight before use.

• CONTAINERS •

Sterilise 1 ℓ + 250 ml bottles.
Makes 1,35 ℓ.

LITCHI LIQUEUR

This small, tropical fruit with its delicate flavour makes an exceptionally tasty liqueur.

• **INGREDIENTS** •

500 g fresh litchis
750 ml brandy
600 g (750 ml) sugar
500 ml water

• **METHOD** •

Peel and stone the litchis. Mash the litchis lightly with a potato masher.

Place the litchis in a wide-necked glass container with a lid. Add the brandy, close tightly and leave to stand for five weeks. Shake regularly.

Strain the mixture through cheesecloth. Set aside.

Mix the sugar and water in a heavy-bottomed pot and stir until the sugar has melted. Bring to the boil and boil for 18 minutes. Remove the syrup from the stove and leave to cool. Add the flavoured brandy to the cold syrup.

Pour the liqueur into the dry, sterilised bottle, cork, seal and mark. Store for at least a week before use.

• **CONTAINERS** •

Sterilise 1 ℓ bottle.
Makes 1,15 ℓ.

LOQUAT LIQUEUR

This small, sweet-sour fruit, mixed with the cinnamon, leaves a mysterious taste in the mouth!

• **INGREDIENTS** •

500 g fresh loquats
450 g (560 ml) sugar
3 ml ground
  cinnamon
750 ml cane spirit

• **METHOD** •

Wash and halve the loquats. Stone and cut into small pieces.

Place the loquats, sugar and cinnamon in a clean, dry glass or earthenware container with a tightly-fitting lid. Add the cane, close and leave to stand for about eight weeks in a warm spot. Shake every day.

Pour the mixture first through a clean, dry sieve and then strain through cheesecloth. Pour the liqueur into the dry, sterilised bottle, cork, seal and mark. Store for at least two months before use.

• **CONTAINERS** •

Sterilise 1 ℓ bottle.
Makes 1 ℓ.

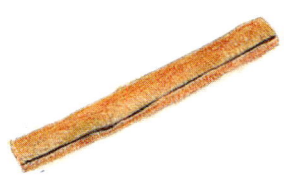

LOVE LIQUEUR

Amor was the Roman god of love. According to legend, this liqueur was a gift from the gods. True or false? We will never know but we do know that it tastes heavenly!

• INGREDIENTS •

300 g violets
1 clove
3 whole allspice
4 cm piece of cassia
1 piece of mace
1 star aniseed
600 g (750 ml) sugar
750 ml water
1 ℓ vodka

• METHOD •

Place the violets and spices in a pot. Add the sugar and water and stir over a very low temperature until the sugar has melted. Bring to the boil and boil until the syrup has discoloured. Remove the syrup from the stove and leave to cool.

Pour the cold syrup into a clean glass container with a tight-fitting lid. Add the vodka, close and leave to stand for a week in a warm spot. Shake every morning and evening.

Strain the mixture through cheesecloth, repeating if necessary. Pour the liqueur into the dry, sterilised bottles, cork, seal and mark. Store for a month before use.

• CONTAINERS •

Sterilise 2 x 750 ml bottles. Makes 1,4 ℓ.

Photograph on p 42

MANGO LIQUEUR

When you think of a mango, you should immediately also think of fenugreek seed – the one is lost without the other. Truly an excellent combination!

• INGREDIENTS •

700 g mango
5 ml bruised
  fenugreek
750 ml cane spirit
600 g (750 ml) sugar
750 ml water

• METHOD •

Peel and cut the mango into small pieces.

Place the mango and fenugreek in a clean, wide-necked glass flask with a lid. Add the cane and close tightly. Leave to stand for a month in a warm spot. Shake every morning and evening.

Pour the mixture first through a clean sieve and then strain through cheesecloth. Set aside.

Mix the sugar and water in a heavy-bottomed pot and stir over a very low temperature until the sugar has melted. Bring to the boil and boil for 16 minutes. Remove the syrup from the stove and leave to cool. Add the flavoured cane to the cold syrup.

Pour the liqueur into the dry, sterilised bottles, cork, seal and mark. Store for a month before use.

• CONTAINERS •

Sterilise 1 ℓ + 250 ml bottles. Makes 1,2 ℓ.

MARULA LIQUEUR

Have you ever wondered why baboons and elephants are so infatuated with marulas? This liqueur will let you into the secret.

• INGREDIENTS •

800 g marulas
750 ml vodka
5 ml fenugreek
4 whole allspice
500 g (625 ml) sugar
650 ml water

• METHOD •

Peel the marulas.

Place the marulas, vodka, fenugreek and allspice in a clean, dry glass or earthenware container with a tight-fitting lid. Leave to stand in a warm spot for three weeks. Shake every morning and evening.

Pour the mixture first through a clean, dry sieve and then strain through two layers of cheesecloth. Set aside.

Mix the sugar and water in a heavy-bottomed pot and stir over a low temperature until the sugar has melted. Bring to the boil and boil for 17 minutes. Remove the syrup from the stove and leave to cool. Mix the syrup with the marula mixture.

Pour the liqueur into the dry, sterilised bottles, cork, seal and mark. Store for a month before use.

• CONTAINERS •

Sterilise 1 ℓ bottle.
Makes 1,15 ℓ.

MULBERRY LIQUEUR

When the children come and show you the first silkworms of the season, you know the time is ripe to place your order for mulberries with those lucky enough to have mulberry trees.

• INGREDIENTS •

500 g mulberries
4 cm piece of stick cinnamon
2 cardamom seeds
1 clove
500 g (625 ml) sugar
750 ml white rum

• METHOD •

Remove the stems from the mulberries. Place the mulberries in a clean glass bowl and mash with a potato masher.

Place the mulberries, spices and sugar in a clean glass or earthenware container with a lid. Add the rum, close tightly and leave to stand for two months. Shake every morning and evening.

Pour the mixture through a clean sieve, pressing out as much rum as possible.

Pour the liqueur into the dry, sterilised bottle, cork, seal and mark. Store for six weeks before use.

• CONTAINERS •

Sterilise 1 ℓ bottle.
Makes 1,15 ℓ.

MUSKMELON LIQUEUR (1)

With the first draught you will congratulate yourself on the unique taste of this liqueur.

• **INGREDIENTS** •

500 g muskmelon
3 cloves
5 cardamom seeds
4 cm piece of stick cinnamon
750 ml witblits
600 g (750 ml) sugar
750 ml water

• **METHOD** •

Halve, peel, seed and cut the melon into pieces.

Place the melon, cloves, cardamom and cinnamon in a clean glass flask with a lid. Add the witblits, close tightly and shake well. Leave to stand in a warm spot for two months. Shake every morning and evening.

Pour the mixture first through a clean sieve and then strain through three layers of cheesecloth. Set aside.

Mix the sugar and water in a heavy-bottomed pot and stir until the sugar has melted. Bring to the boil and boil for 20 minutes. Remove the syrup from the stove and leave to cool. Add the flavoured witblits to the cold syrup.

Pour the liqueur into the dry, sterilised bottle, cork, seal and mark. Store for a month before use.

• **CONTAINERS** •

Sterilise 1 ℓ bottle.
Makes 1 ℓ.

MUSKMELON LIQUEUR (2)

The ginger used in this recipe gives this light-green liqueur a piquant flavour.

• **INGREDIENTS** •

500 g muskmelon
5 cm piece of fresh ginger root
200 g (250 ml) sugar
750 ml vodka

• **METHOD** •

Halve, peel, seed and cut the melon into pieces. Peel and cut the ginger into small pieces.

Place the melon, ginger and sugar in a clean glass or earthenware container with a tight-fitting lid. Add the vodka, shake well and leave to stand for a month in a warm spot. Shake very well twice a day.

Pour the mixture first through a clean sieve and then strain through three layers of cheesecloth. Pour the liqueur into the dry, sterilised bottle, cork, seal and mark. Store for a month before use.

• **CONTAINERS** •

Sterilise 1 ℓ bottle.
Makes 850 ml.

NAARTJIE LIQUEUR

Winter time is naartjie time. Ask the children not to throw away their naartjie peels. You can use either fresh or dry peels.

• INGREDIENTS •

35 ml naartjie peel
3 cloves
4 cm piece of stick cinnamon
1 piece of whole mace
750 ml witblits
60 ml rum
300 g (375 ml) sugar
200 ml water

• METHOD •

Remove the pith from the inside of the peel and cut the peel into pieces.

Place the peel, cloves, cinnamon and mace in a dry glass or earthenware container with a lid. Add the witblits and rum, close tightly and shake well. Leave to stand for a month in a warm spot. Shake every morning and evening.

Pour the mixture first through a clean, dry sieve and then through two layers of cheesecloth. Set aside.

Mix the sugar and water in a heavy-bottomed pot and stir until the sugar has melted. Bring to the boil and boil for 15 minutes. Remove the syrup from the stove and leave to cool. Add the flavoured witblits to the cold syrup.

Pour the liqueur into the dry, sterilised bottle, cork, seal and mark. Store for at least a fortnight before use.

• CONTAINERS •

Sterilise 1 x 750 ml + 250 ml bottles.
Makes 950 ml.

ORANGE BLOSSOM LIQUEUR

For the flavour of the orange blossoms to mix fully with that of the brandy, no spices are used.

• INGREDIENTS •

200 g orange blossom
750 ml brandy
600 g (750 ml) sugar
750 ml water

• METHOD •

Wash the blossoms thoroughly, place on clean, dry cheesecloth, fold closed and shake to remove the water. Bruise the blossoms lightly.

Place the blossoms in a clean, dry wide-necked glass container with a screw lid. Add the brandy, close and shake well. Leave to stand for 15 days in a warm spot. Shake every morning and evening.

Strain the mixture through two layers of cheesecloth. Set aside.

Mix the sugar and water in a heavy-bottomed pot and stir over a very low temperature until the sugar has melted. Bring to the boil and boil for 17 minutes. Remove the syrup from the stove and leave to cool. Add the flavoured brandy to the cold syrup.

Pour the liqueur into the dry, sterilised bottle, cork, seal and mark. Store for at least a month before use.

• CONTAINERS •

Sterilise 1 ℓ bottle.
Makes 1,15 ℓ.

ORANGE LIQUEUR (1)

Oranges are available almost throughout the year; nothing therefore prevents you from regularly treating your guests to an orange liqueur.

• **INGREDIENTS** •

10 oranges
500 g (625 ml) sugar
5 cm piece of stick cinnamon
5 ml whole coriander
750 ml brandy

• **METHOD** •

Peel the oranges thinly.

Mix the peel, sugar, cinnamon and coriander, place in a wide-necked glass flask with a tightly-fitting lid. Add the brandy, close and shake well. Leave to stand for eight weeks in a warm spot. Shake twice a day.

Strain the mixture through cheesecloth. Pour the liqueur into the dry, sterilised bottles, cork, seal and mark. Store for a week before use.

• **CONTAINERS** •

Sterilise 1 ℓ bottle.
Makes 1 ℓ.

ORANGE LIQUEUR (2)

The temptation to clean your glass with your finger so that nothing of this delicious liqueur is lost will be near irresistible!

• **INGREDIENTS** •

5 oranges
3 lemons
5 cloves
750 ml witblits
750 g (940 ml) sugar
750 ml water

• **METHOD** •

Peel the oranges and lemons very thinly with a vegetable peeler.

Place the peels and cloves in a glass or earthenware container with a lid. Add the witblits, close tightly and leave to stand for a fortnight in a warm spot. Shake every day.

Strain the mixture through cheesecloth. Set aside.

Mix the sugar and water in a heavy-bottomed pot and stir until the sugar has melted. Bring to the boil and boil for 17 minutes. Remove the syrup from the stove and leave to cool. Add the flavoured witblits to the cold syrup.

Pour the liqueur into the dry, sterilised bottle, cork, seal and mark. Store for a month before use.

• **CONTAINERS** •

Sterilise 1 x 750 ml + 500 ml bottles.
Makes 1,5 ℓ

Photograph on p 52

ORANGE LIQUEUR (3)

An interesting sweet-sour combination.

• INGREDIENTS •

2 Seville oranges
3 Valencia oranges
250 g (300 ml) sugar
750 ml gin

• METHOD •

Peel the oranges very thinly, cut the peel into pieces and squeeze the juice into a jug. Pour the juice through a sieve to remove the pips and fibres.

Place the peel, juice and sugar in a clean glass or earthenware container with a lid. Add the gin and stir until the sugar has melted. Close the container tightly and leave to stand for a month. Shake every day.

Strain the mixture through cheesecloth. Pour the liqueur into the dry, sterilised bottle, cork, seal and mark. Store for six months in a cool spot before use.

• CONTAINERS •

Sterilise 1 x 750 ml bottle.
Makes 875 ml.

PAPINO LIQUEUR

The flesh of the papino is sweet and is orange-pink in colour.

• INGREDIENTS •

700 g papino
1 vanilla pod
3 allspice pepper corns
750 ml vodka
500 g (625 ml) sugar
650 ml water

• METHOD •

Peel, halve, stone and cut the papino into pieces. Cut the vanilla pod lengthways and break into smaller pieces.

Place the papino, vanilla and allspice in a clean, dry glass or earthenware container with a lid. Add the vodka, close tightly and leave to stand in a warm spot. Shake every day.

Pour the mixture first through a clean sieve and then strain through two layers of cheesecloth. Set aside.

Mix the sugar and water in a heavy-bottomed pot and stir over a very low temperature until the sugar has melted. Bring to the boil and boil for 16 minutes. Remove the syrup from the stove and leave to cool. Add the flavoured vodka to the cold syrup.

Pour the liqueur into the dry, sterilised bottles, cork, seal and mark. Store for a month before use.

• CONTAINERS •

Sterilise 1 ℓ + 250 ml bottles.
Makes 1,25 ℓ.

PEACH LEAF LIQUEUR

Early in September the leaves of the peach trees are still young – therefore the ideal time to make peach leaf liqueur.

• **INGREDIENTS** •

20 g young peach leaves
50 g almonds, shelled
1 piece of mace
750 ml brandy
600 g (750 ml) sugar
750 ml water

• **METHOD** •

Wash and dry the leaves thoroughly. Chop up the almonds.
 Place the leaves, almonds and mace in a glass or earthenware container with a lid. Add the brandy, close and shake well. Leave to stand for a month in a warm spot. Shake regularly.
 Strain the mixture through cheesecloth. Set aside.
 Mix the sugar and water in a heavy-bottomed pot and stir until the sugar has melted. Bring to the boil and boil for 17 minutes. Remove the syrup from the stove and leave to cool. Add the flavoured brandy to the cold syrup.
 Pour the liqueur into the dry, sterilised bottles, cork, seal and mark. Store for a month before use.

• **CONTAINERS** •

Sterilise 1 ℓ bottle.
Makes 1,15 ℓ.

PEACH LIQUEUR (1)

Use clingstone peaches but remember to retain the stones.

• **INGREDIENTS** •

500 g fresh peaches
300 g (375 ml) sugar
2 pieces of mace
750 ml brandy

• **METHOD** •

Halve, stone and slice the peaches. Crack the stones, remove the kernels and pull off the skins.
 Arrange the peaches and sugar in alternate layers in a glass or earthenware container with a tightly-fitting lid. Add the mace, brandy and kernels, close and leave to stand for three weeks in a warm spot. Shake every day.
 Strain the mixture through cheesecloth into a glass bowl. Pour the liqueur into the dry, sterilised bottles, cork, seal and mark. Store for at least a month before use.

• **CONTAINERS** •

Sterilise 1 ℓ bottle.
Makes 950 ml.

PEACH LIQUEUR (2)

The tot of rum that is added lends a mysterious flavour to this liqueur.

• INGREDIENTS •

peach stones
500 g fresh peach slices
5 ml allspice
500 g (625 ml) sugar
750 ml dry white wine
50 ml rum
500 ml vodka

• METHOD •

Crack the stones and remove the kernels.

Place the peaches, allspice and sugar in a pot. Add the wine and stir over a low temperature until the sugar has melted. Bring to the boil and boil to just before the peaches are soft. Spoon off the foam. Remove from the stove, leave to cool slightly and add the rum, vodka and kernels. Pour into a dry glass or earthenware container, close tightly and leave to stand for a fortnight in a warm spot. Shake every morning and evening.

Pour the mixture first through a dry, clean sieve and then strain through four layers of cheesecloth. Pour the liqueur into the dry, sterilised bottles, cork, seal and mark. Store for a week before use.

• CONTAINERS •

Sterilise 2 x 750 ml bottles.
Makes 1,5 ℓ.

PEACH STONE LIQUEUR

Why throw away the stones if you can use them?

• INGREDIENTS •

14 peach stones
20 peach leaves
1 piece of mace
750 ml brandy
500 g (625 ml) sugar
650 ml water

• METHOD •

Crack the stones and remove the kernels. Pull off the skins and cut into pieces. Wash and dry the leaves.

Place the kernels, leaves and mace in a clean glass or earthenware container with a tightly-fitting lid. Add the brandy and close tightly. Leave to stand for a month in a warm spot. Shake every morning and evening.

Strain the mixture through cheesecloth. Set aside.

Mix the sugar and water in a heavy-bottomed pot and stir until the sugar has melted. Bring to the boil and boil for 17 minutes. Remove the syrup from the stove and leave to cool. Add the flavoured brandy to the cold syrup.

Pour the liqueur into the dry, sterilised bottle, cork, seal and mark. Store for at least two months before use.

• CONTAINERS •

Sterilise 1 ℓ bottle.
Makes 1,15 ℓ.

PEAR LIQUEUR

Nothing tastes better than pears stewed with cloves - except this liqueur!

• INGREDIENTS •

500 g fresh table pears
5 whole cloves
2 cm piece of ginger root, peeled
500 g (625 ml) sugar
500 ml dry white wine
500 ml gin

• METHOD •

Halve, seed and slice the pears.

Place the pears, cloves, ginger and sugar in a heavy-bottomed pot. Add the wine. Heat over a low temperature and stir until the sugar has melted. Bring to the boil. Remove the syrup from the stove and leave to cool.

Add the gin to the cold syrup. Pour the mixture into a clean glass or earthenware container, close tightly and leave to stand for a week in a warm spot. Shake every morning and evening.

Strain the mixture through two layers of cheesecloth, repeating if necessary.

Pour the liqueur into the dry, sterilised bottle, cork, seal and mark. Store for a month before use.

• CONTAINERS •

Sterilise 1 ℓ bottle.
Makes 1,05 ℓ.

PEEL LIQUEUR

The most important ingredient of this liqueur is the peel of a lime and a lemon - hence the name.

• INGREDIENTS •

1 lime
1 lemon
1 sprig of rosemary
100 g orange blossom
3 cloves
750 ml vodka
600 g (750 ml) sugar
750 ml water

• METHOD •

Grate the lime and lemon peel carefully - do not grate the pith. Bruise the rosemary and orange blossom.

Place the peel, rosemary, orange blossom and cloves in a clean, dry glass flask with a lid. Add the vodka, close tightly and leave to stand for three weeks in a warm spot. Shake every morning and evening.

Strain the mixture through cheesecloth, repeating if necessary. Set aside.

Mix the sugar and water in a heavy-bottomed pot and stir until the sugar has melted. Heat over a very low temperature, bring to the boil and boil for 17 minutes. Remove the syrup from the stove and leave to cool. Add the flavoured vodka to the cold syrup.

Pour the liqueur into the dry, sterilised bottles, cork, seal and mark. Store for a month before use.

• CONTAINERS •

Sterilise 1 x 750 ml + 500 ml bottles.
Makes 1,15 ℓ.

Photograph on p 17

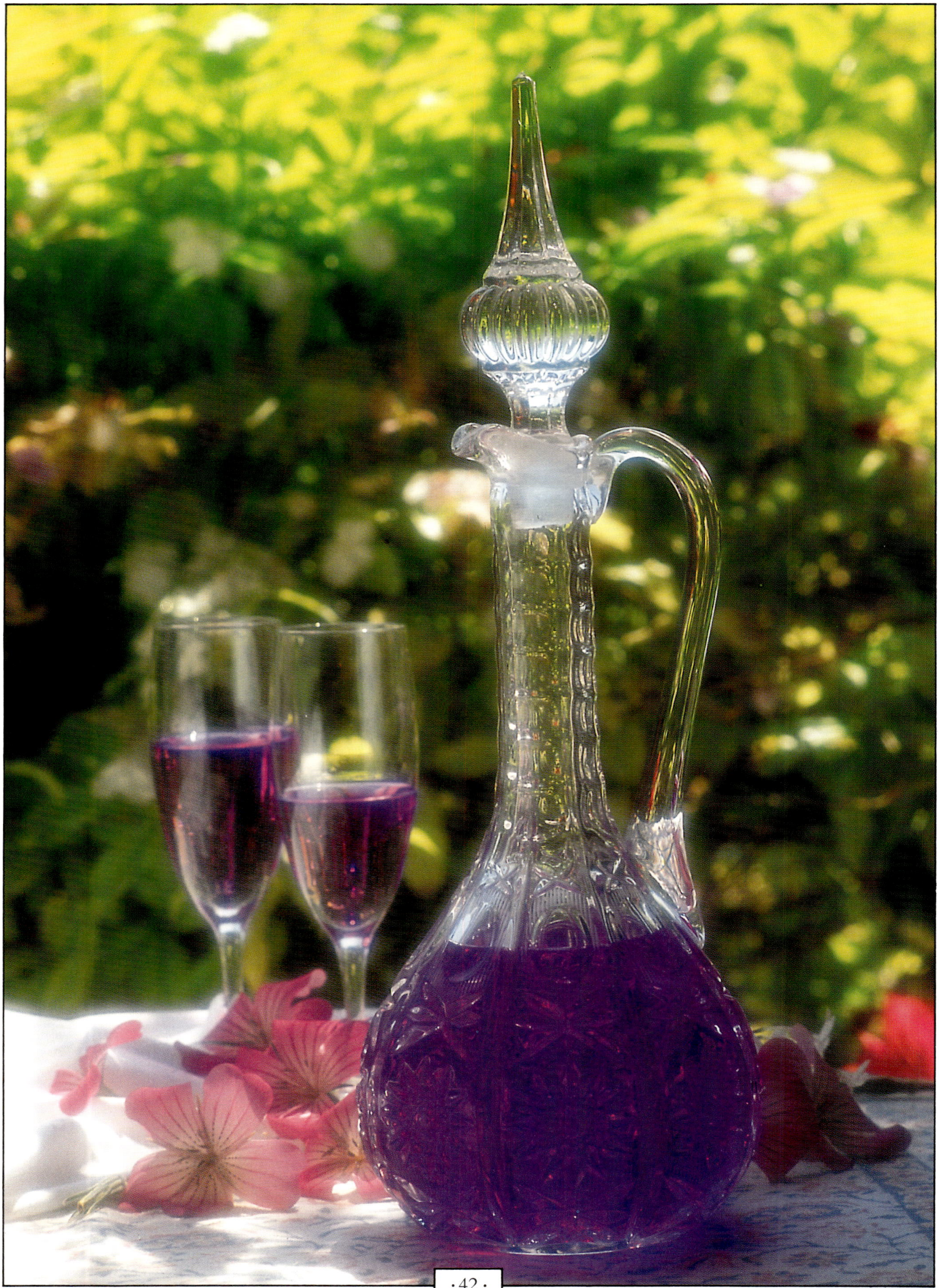

PINEAPPLE LIQUEUR (1)

Nicer than nice – a perfect description of this yellow liqueur.

• **INGREDIENTS** •

500 g pineapple, peeled
200 g (250 ml) sugar
4 cloves
1 piece of stick cinnamon
750 ml brandy

• **METHOD** •

Remove all the eyes from the peeled pineapple. Grate or pulp the pineapple in a food processor.

Place the pineapple, sugar, cloves and cinnamon in a clean, dry glass or earthenware container with a lid. Add the brandy, close and shake well. Leave to stand for at least seven weeks in a warm spot. Shake every day.

Pour the mixture first through a clean, dry sieve and then strain through cheesecloth. Pour the liqueur into the dry, sterilised bottles, cork, seal and mark. Store for eight weeks before use.

• **CONTAINERS** •

Sterilise 1 x 750 ml + 500 ml bottles.
Makes 850 ml.

PINEAPPLE LIQUEUR (2)

The taste of this liqueur will take you away to a tropical island where the sun never sets ...

• **INGREDIENTS** •

500 g pineapple, peeled
150 g (175 ml) sugar
1 ℓ gin
30 ml white rum

• **METHOD** •

Remove all the eyes from the peeled pineapple. Grate or pulp the pineapple in a food processor.

Place the pineapple and sugar in a glass or earthenware container with a lid. Add the gin and rum. Close tightly, shake well and leave to stand for at least two months in a warm spot. Shake regularly.

Strain through cheesecloth.

Pour the liqueur into the dry, sterilised bottles, cork, seal and mark. Store for a week before use.

• **CONTAINERS** •

Sterilise 1 ℓ bottle.
Makes 1,05 ℓ.

PINEAPPLE LIQUEUR (3)

If pineapple peel is good enough for pineapple beer, why not also for pineapple liqueur?

• INGREDIENTS •

peel of 2 pineapples
2,5 ml ground ginger
750 ml brandy
600 g (750 ml) sugar
750 ml water

• METHOD •

Place the peel and ginger in a clean, dry container with a tightly-fitting lid. Add the brandy, close and shake well. Leave to stand for about a month in a warm spot. Shake every morning and evening.

Pour the mixture first through a clean sieve and then strain through cheesecloth. Set aside.

Mix the sugar and water in a heavy-bottomed pot and stir until the sugar has melted. Bring to the boil and boil for 20 minutes. Remove the syrup from the stove and leave to cool. Add the flavoured brandy to the cold syrup.

Pour the liqueur into the dry, sterilised bottle, cork, seal and mark. Store for a fortnight before use.

• CONTAINERS •

Sterilise 1 x 750 ml + 500 ml bottles. Makes 1,15 ℓ.

PLUM LIQUEUR (1)

The colour of this liqueur depends on the type of plums you use - it can vary from light-red to deep-purple.

• INGREDIENTS •

500 g fresh plums
200 g (250 ml) sugar
750 ml gin
50 ml white rum

• METHOD •

Halve, stone and cut the plums into small pieces.

Place the plums and sugar in a glass or earthenware container with a tightly-fitting lid. Add the gin and rum, close tightly and leave to stand for a month in a warm spot. Shake regularly.

Pour the mixture first through a clean, dry sieve and then strain through two layers of cheesecloth. Pour the liqueur into the dry, sterilised bottle, cork, seal and mark. Store for a month before use.

• CONTAINERS •

Sterilise 1 ℓ bottle. Makes 900 ml.

PLUM LIQUEUR (2)

For this recipe, use the Santa Rosa plums - the type with the characteristic deep-red colour.

• INGREDIENTS •

500 g fresh plums
500 g (625 ml) sugar
750 ml gin
2 drops of almond essence

• METHOD •

Prick the plums with a fork.

Place the plums and sugar in a glass or earthenware container with a tightly-fitting lid. Close and shake well to mix the plum juice and sugar. Leave to stand for four days in a warm spot. Add the gin and essence, close tightly and leave to stand for two months. Shake regularly.

Remove the plums and strain the mixture through three layers of cheesecloth. Pour the liqueur into the dry, sterilised bottle, cork, seal and mark. Store for a month before use.

• CONTAINERS •

Sterilise 1 ℓ bottle.
Makes 1 ℓ.

POMEGRANATE LIQUEUR

The pomegranate is a fruit that is very much neglected and even forgotten. It makes a bright-red liqueur.

• INGREDIENTS •

500 g pomegranate pips
1 ml grated lemon peel
2 cardamom seeds
750 ml vodka
500 g (625 ml) sugar
600 ml water

• METHOD •

Halve a pomegranate and remove the juicy red pips.

Place the pips, peel, and cardamom in a clean glass flask with a tightly-fitting lid. Add the vodka, stir thoroughly and close. Leave to stand for 10 days in a warm spot. Shake at least twice a day.

Strain the mixture through cheesecloth. Set aside.

Mix the sugar and water in a heavy-bottomed pot and stir until the sugar has melted. Bring to the boil and boil for 18 minutes. Remove the syrup from the stove and leave to cool. Add the flavoured vodka to the cold syrup.

Pour the liqueur into the dry, sterilised bottles, cork, seal and mark. Store for at least two months before use.

• CONTAINERS •

Sterilise 1 x 750 ml + 500 ml bottles.
Makes 1,15 ℓ.

RED ROSE PETAL LIQUEUR

The delicate flavour and blood-red petals of the roses used in this recipe make the liqueur a winner. Use only roses with a strong scent.

• **INGREDIENTS** •

25 red roses
750 ml witblits
600 g (750 ml) sugar
500 ml water

• **METHOD** •

Wash the roses carefully and remove the petals.

Place the petals in a wide-necked glass or earthenware container with a lid. Add the witblits, close and leave to stand for six weeks in a warm spot. Shake regularly.

Strain the mixture through cheesecloth until clear. Set aside.

Mix the sugar and water in a heavy-bottomed pot and stir until the sugar has melted. Bring to the boil and boil for 18 minutes. Remove the syrup from the stove and leave to cool. Add the flavoured witblits to the cold syrup.

Pour the liqueur into the dry, sterilised bottles, cork, seal and mark. Store for two months before use.

• **CONTAINERS** •

Sterilise 1 x 750 ml + 500 ml bottles. Makes 1,15 ℓ.

RHUBARB LIQUEUR

Rhubarb, with its long, pink stem, is actually a vegetable.

• **INGREDIENTS** •

500 g fresh rhubarb
5 cm piece of stick cinnamon
2 cloves
500 g (625 ml) sugar
750 ml dry white wine
500 ml vodka

• **METHOD** •

Cut the rhubarb into small pieces.

Place the rhubarb, cinnamon, cloves and sugar in a pot. Add the wine. Stir over a low temperature until the sugar has melted. Bring to the boil. Remove from the stove and leave to cool well.

Pour the vodka into a clean, dry glass or earthenware container with a lid. Add the rhubarb mixture. Close the container tightly and leave to stand for three weeks in a warm spot. Shake every morning and evening.

Strain the mixture through cheesecloth, repeating until clear and transparent.

Pour the liqueur into the dry, sterilised bottles, cork, seal and mark. Store for a month before use.

• **CONTAINERS** •

Sterilise 2 x 750 ml bottles. Makes 1,5 ℓ.

SEVILLE ORANGE LIQUEUR

This type of orange has a bitter taste and is used to make marmalade. Its flesh is deep-yellow - hence the attractive colour of the liqueur.

• **INGREDIENTS** •

40 sugar cubes
4 big Seville oranges
750 ml white rum

• **METHOD** •

Rub the sugar cubes over the peel of the oranges until dark-orange (the sugar absorbs the oil in the peel). Peel the oranges, remove the pith from the flesh and cut into pieces.

Place the orange and sugar in a glass container with a lid. Add the rum, close and leave to stand for two months in a warm spot. Shake every morning and evening.

Pour the mixture first through a sieve and then strain through cheesecloth. Pour the liqueur into the dry, sterilised bottle, cork, seal and mark. Store for a month before use.

• **CONTAINERS** •

Sterilise 1 ℓ bottle. Makes 850 ml.

STRAWBERRY LIQUEUR (1)

Even a beginner will be proud of the end product - a deep-red liqueur.

• **INGREDIENTS** •

500 g fresh strawberries
1 ml black pepper
750 ml gin
200 g (250 ml) sugar
200 ml dry white wine

• **METHOD** •

Wash the strawberries, remove the leaves and stems and cut into quarters.

Place the strawberries and black pepper in a clean, dry glass or earthenware container with a lid and add the gin.

Mix the sugar and wine in a heavy-bottomed pot and stir over a low temperature until the sugar has dissolved. Bring to the boil and boil for 7 minutes. Remove the syrup from the stove and leave to cool. Add the cold syrup to the strawberry mixture. Close tightly and leave to stand for a fortnight in a warm spot. Shake every morning and evening.

Pour the mixture first through a dry, clean sieve and then strain through two layers of cheesecloth.

Pour the liqueur into the dry, sterilised bottle, cork, seal and mark. Store for at least a month before use.

• **CONTAINERS** •

Sterilise 1 ℓ bottle. Makes 950 ml.

STRAWBERRY LIQUEUR (2)

A (literally) breathtaking liqueur! The witblits base gives it slightly more of a kick than the previous strawberry liqueur – a challenge to the strong among us!

• **INGREDIENTS** •

500 g strawberries
1 ml black pepper
750 ml witblits
600 g (750 ml) sugar
750 ml water

• **METHOD** •

Wash the strawberries, remove the leaves and stems and halve.

Place the strawberries and pepper in a clean, wide-necked container with a screw lid. Add the witblits, close tightly and leave to stand for a month in a warm spot.

Pour the mixture first through a clean, dry sieve and then strain through two layers of cheesecloth. Set aside.

Mix the sugar and water in a heavy-bottomed pot and stir well over a low temperature until the sugar has melted. Bring to the boil and boil for 17 minutes. Remove the syrup from the stove and leave to cool. Add the flavoured witblits to the cold syrup.

Pour the liqueur into the dry, sterilised bottles, cork, seal and mark. Store for a month before use.

• **CONTAINERS** •

Sterilise 1 x 750 ml + 500 ml bottles. Makes 1,1 ℓ.

SWEET MELON LIQUEUR

Use the variety with the ribbed rind and orange flesh.

• **INGREDIENTS** •

1 kg sweet melon
3 cm piece of fresh ginger root
5 cardamom seeds
750 ml white rum
500 g (625 ml) sugar
650 ml water

• **METHOD** •

Halve, seed, peel and cut the melon into small pieces. Slice the ginger thinly.

Place the melon, ginger and cardamom into a clean, wide-necked glass flask with a lid. Add the rum, close tightly and leave to stand for three weeks in a warm spot. Shake every morning and evening.

Pour the mixture first through a clean, dry sieve and then strain through cheesecloth. Set aside.

Mix the sugar and water in a heavy-bottomed pot and stir until the sugar has melted. Heat over a very low temperature, bring to the boil and boil for 16 minutes. Remove the syrup from the stove and leave to cool. Add the flavoured rum to the cold syrup.

Pour the liqueur into the dry, sterilised bottles, cork, seal and mark. Store for a month before use.

• **CONTAINERS** •

Sterilise 2 x 750 ml bottles. Makes 1,45 ℓ.

TROPICAL LIQUEUR

A mixture of tropical fruit, spices and rum gives a real Caribbean flavour to this liqueur.

• INGREDIENTS •

150 g fresh pineapple
100 g fresh guava
100 g papino
150 g (175 ml) sugar
2 cardamom seeds
5 ml allspice
150 ml gin
30 ml rum
30 ml brandy

• METHOD •

Peel the fruit. Remove the core of the pineapple. Seed the guava and papino. Cut the fruit into pieces and pulp in a food processor.

Place the pulp, sugar, cardamom and allspice in a big glass container with a screw lid. Add the gin, rum and brandy. Close, shake and leave to stand for two months in a warm spot. Shake every morning and evening.

Strain the mixture through cheesecloth, repeating if necessary. Pour the liqueur into the dry, sterilised bottle, cork, seal and mark. Store for three weeks before use.

• CONTAINERS •

Sterilise 1 ℓ bottle.
Makes 850 ml.

VAN DER HUM LIQUEUR

This liqueur has its origins in South Africa. With time, the recipe, just like a good piece of gossip, has undergone many changes – but only for the best!

• INGREDIENTS •

750 ml brandy
50 ml rum
4 cardamom seeds
4 cm piece of stick cinnamon
4 cloves
3 ml ground nutmeg
30 ml naartjie peel
300 g (375 ml) sugar
200 ml water

• METHOD •

Pour the brandy and rum into a glass or earthenware container with a lid. Add the cardamom, cinnamon, cloves and nutmeg. Remove the pith from the naartjie peel and add the peel to the mixture. Close tightly, shake thoroughly and leave to stand for a month in a warm spot. Shake every day.

Pour the mixture first through a clean sieve and then strain through cheesecloth. Set aside.

Mix the sugar and water in a heavy-bottomed pot and stir until the sugar has melted. Heat over a very low temperature, bring to the boil and boil for 15 minutes. Remove the syrup from the stove and leave to cool. Add the flavoured brandy to the cold syrup.

Pour the liqueur into the dry, sterilised bottles, cork, seal and mark. Store for a fortnight before use.

• CONTAINERS •

Sterilise 1 ℓ bottle.
Makes 1 ℓ.

Photograph on p 60

VANILLA LIQUEUR

Vanilla is an important ingredient in many desserts and sweet cakes. The pods are ideal for a liqueur.

• INGREDIENTS •

2 vanilla pods
750 ml vodka
600 g (750 ml) sugar
600 ml water

• METHOD •

Cut the vanilla pods lengthways and break into smaller pieces. Place in a clean, dry glass or earthenware container with a lid. Add the vodka, close and shake regularly. Leave to stand for a month in a warm spot. Shake regularly.

Strain the mixture through cheesecloth. Set aside.

Mix the sugar and water in a heavy-bottomed pot and stir until the sugar has melted. Bring to the boil and boil for 17 minutes. Remove the syrup from the stove and leave to cool. Add the flavoured vodka to the cold syrup.

Pour the liqueur into the dry, sterilised bottles, cork, seal and mark. Store for a month before use.

• CONTAINERS •

Sterilise 1 ℓ + 500 ml bottles.
Makes 1,15 ℓ.

VERBENA LIQUEUR

Refreshing, different, definitely lemon - a true description of this liqueur.

• INGREDIENTS •

250 ml dry white wine
2 x 4 cm sprigs of verbena
2 x 3 cm sprigs of rosemary
4 cardamom seeds
4 whole allspice
750 ml witblits
600 g (750 ml) sugar
750 ml water

• METHOD •

Heat the wine. Bruise the verbena and rosemary and add the wine. Bring to the boil. Remove from the stove and leave to cool.

Pour the mixture into a clean, wide-necked glass flask with a lid. Add the cardamom, allspice and witblits. Close tightly and leave to stand for three days in a warm spot. Shake at least once a day.

Strain the mixture through a few layers of cheesecloth until clear and transparent. Set aside.

Mix the sugar and water in a heavy-bottomed pot and stir until the sugar has melted. Heat over a very low temperature, bring to the boil and boil for 17 minutes. Remove the syrup from the stove and leave to cool. Add the flavoured witblits to the cold syrup.

Pour the liqueur into the dry, sterilised bottles, cork, seal and mark. Store for two months before use.

• CONTAINERS •

Sterilise 2 x 750 ml bottles.
Makes 1,4 ℓ.

VIOLET LIQUEUR

Although this liqueur is named after the flower it is, in fact, music on the tongue!

• INGREDIENTS •

300 g violets
250 ml dry white wine
2 cloves
4 whole allspice
3 cm piece of stick cinnamon
1 ℓ white rum
500 g (625 ml) sugar
650 ml water

• METHOD •

Place the violets in a heavy-bottomed pot and add the wine. Bring to the boil. Remove from the stove and leave to cool. Pour the mixture into a glass container with a lid. Add the cloves, allspice, cinnamon and rum. Close tightly and leave to stand for a week in a warm spot. Shake every morning and evening.

Strain the mixture through cheesecloth, repeating if necessary. Set aside.

Mix the sugar and water in a heavy-bottomed pot and stir over a very low temperature until the sugar has melted. Bring to the boil and boil for 15 minutes. Remove the syrup from the stove and leave to cool. Add the flavoured rum to the cold syrup.

Pour the liqueur into the dry, sterilised bottles, cork, seal and mark. Store for a month before use.

• CONTAINERS •

Sterilise 1 ℓ + 750 ml bottles.
Makes 1,65 ℓ.

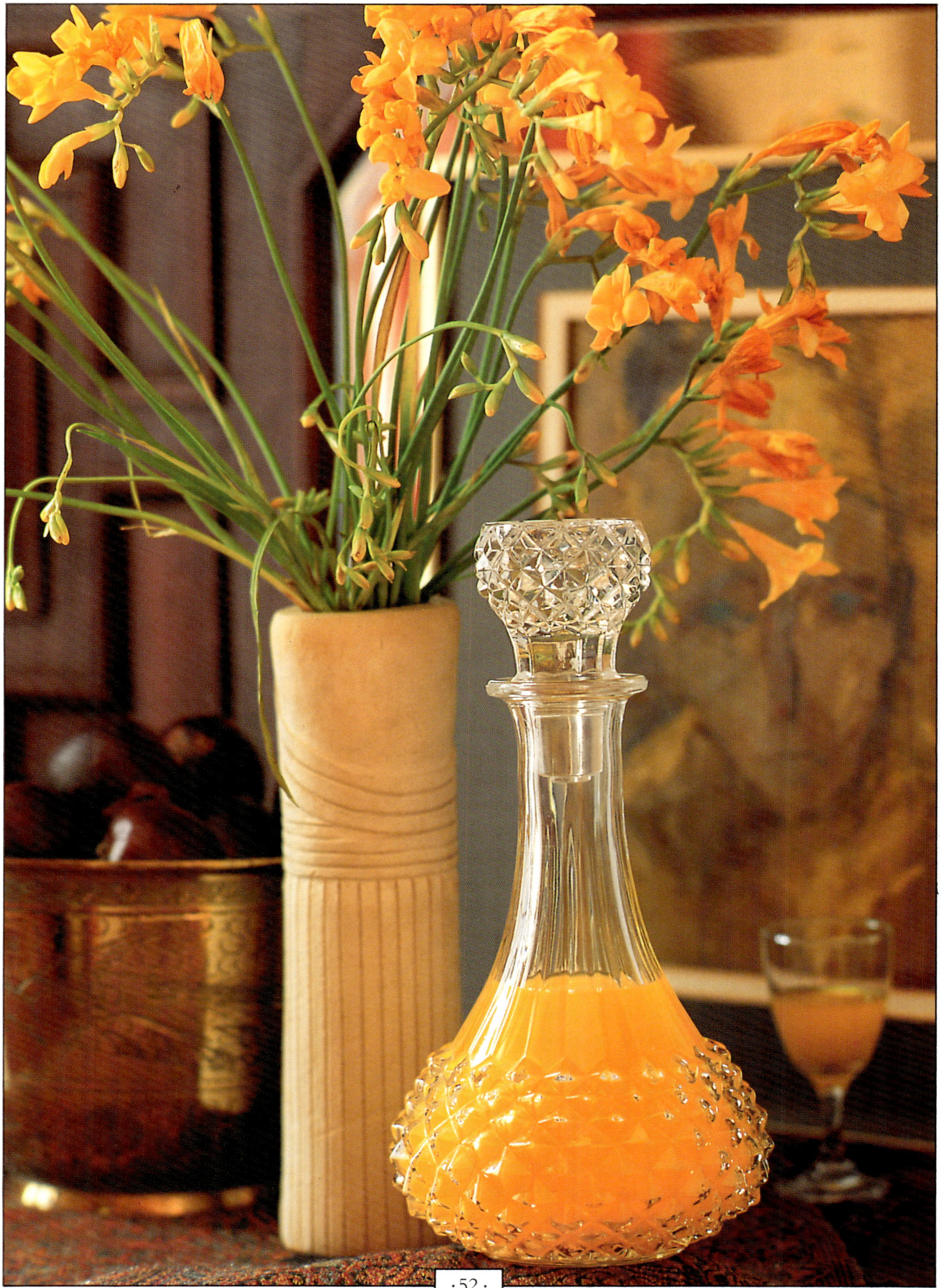

FRUIT CREAM AND INSTANT LIQUEUR

ADVOCAAT LIQUEUR (1)

• INGREDIENTS •

7 eggs
300 g (325 ml) sugar
5 ml vanilla essence
325 ml brandy

• METHOD •

Beat the eggs and sugar until creamy. Pour the mixture, together with the essence, into a double boiler or a glass bowl over boiling water. Stir until the sugar has dissolved and the mixture is light-yellow. Add the brandy slowly, stirring continuously. Boil until the mixture thickens. Remove from the stove and leave to cool.

Pour the liqueur into the dry, sterilised bottles, cork, seal and mark. Refrigerate before use.

• CONTAINERS •

*Sterilise 1 ℓ bottle.
Makes 850 ml.*

ADVOCAAT LIQUEUR (2)

• INGREDIENTS •

300 ml water
150 g (175 ml) sugar
peel of 1 lemon
6 egg yolks
375 ml vodka

• METHOD •

Mix the water, sugar and peel in a pot. Bring to the boil. Remove the syrup from the stove and remove the peel.

Beat the egg until creamy. Add the warm syrup little by little and beat quickly to prevent the egg from curdling. Add the vodka and mix thoroughly.

Pour the liqueur into the dry, sterilised bottles, cork, seal and mark. Refrigerate for a week before use.

• CONTAINERS •

Sterilise 1 ℓ bottle.
Makes 900 ml.

ANISEED CREAM LIQUEUR

• INGREDIENTS •

15 g star aniseed
300 ml brandy
397 g tin of condensed milk
250 ml fresh cream
15 ml glycerine

• METHOD •

Place the aniseed in a dry glass container with a lid. Add the brandy, close, shake and leave to stand for about a fortnight in a warm spot. Shake regularly.

Strain the mixture through cheesecloth. Set aside.

Pour the condensed milk, cream and glycerine into a liquidiser and mix for 15 minutes. Add the flavoured brandy and liquidise for another five minutes.

Pour the liqueur into the dry, sterilised bottles, cork, seal and mark. Refrigerate for 12 hours before use.

• CONTAINERS •

Sterilise 1 ℓ bottle.
Makes 850 ml.

APRICOT CREAM LIQUEUR

• INGREDIENTS •

250 g fresh apricots
1 ml allspice
400 ml dry white wine
300 ml gin
397 g tin of condensed milk
410 g tin of evaporated milk
10 ml glycerine

• METHOD •

Halve and stone the apricots. Crack the stones, remove the kernels and pull off the skins.

Place the apricots, kernels and allspice in a pot and add the wine. Bring to the boil and boil until the apricots are soft. Remove from the stove and leave to cool. Place the mixture into a clean, dry glass flask with a screw lid. Add the gin, close and leave to stand for a week in a warm spot. Shake twice a day.

Pour the mixture first through a clean sieve and then strain through cheesecloth. Pour the flavoured wine and gin into a liquidiser, together with the condensed and evaporated milk and the glycerine, and liquidise for 15 minutes.

Pour the liqueur into the dry, sterilised bottles, cork, seal and mark. Refrigerate for two days before use.

• CONTAINERS •

*Sterilise 1 ℓ bottle.
Makes 850 ml.*

BANANA CREAM LIQUEUR

• INGREDIENTS •

3 ripe bananas
1 ml ground cinnamon
1 ml allspice
300 ml brandy
397 g tin of condensed milk
250 ml fresh cream
10 ml glycerine

• METHOD •

Peel and slice the banana.

Place the banana, cinnamon and allspice in a clean, dry glass flask with a lid. Add the brandy, close, shake and leave to stand for a fortnight in a warm spot. Shake every morning and evening.

Strain the mixture through cheesecloth. Set aside.

Beat the condensed milk, cream and glycerine for 10 minutes in a mixer. Add the flavoured brandy and beat for another two minutes.

Pour the liqueur into the dry, sterilised bottles, cork, seal and mark. Refrigerate for a few days before use.

• CONTAINERS •

*Sterilise 1 ℓ bottle.
Makes 850 ml.*

BLACKBERRY CREAM LIQUEUR

• INGREDIENTS •

250 g fresh blackberries
300 ml witblits
397 g tin of condensed milk
410 g tin of evaporated milk
10 ml glycerine

• METHOD •

Remove the stems from the blackberries.

Place the blackberries in a clean, dry glass container with a screw lid. Add the witblits, close and leave to stand for a fortnight in a warm spot. Shake every morning and evening.

Pour the mixture first through a clean sieve and then strain through two layers of cheesecloth. Set aside.

Pour the condensed and evaporated milk and the glycerine into a liquidiser and mix for 10 minutes. Add the flavoured witblits and mix for another 10 minutes.

Pour the liqueur into the dry, sterilised bottles, cork, seal and mark. Refrigerate for a week before use.

• CONTAINERS •

Sterilise 1 ℓ bottle.
Makes 1 ℓ.

Photograph on p 79

BLUEBERRY CREAM LIQUEUR

• INGREDIENTS •

250 g fresh blueberries
100 ml sweet wine
1 vanilla pod
300 ml red rum
397 g tin of condensed milk
250 ml fresh cream
10 ml glycerine

• METHOD •

Remove the stems and halve the blueberries.

Place the blueberries in a pot and add the sweet wine. Bring to the boil and remove from the stove. Break the vanilla pod into pieces and add to the mixture. Leave to cool. Pour into a glass container with a lid and add the rum. Close and leave to stand for about a week in a warm spot. Shake every morning and evening.

Strain the mixture through cheesecloth into a glass bowl. Set aside.

Pour the condensed milk, cream and glycerine into a mixer or liquidiser and mix thoroughly.

Pour the liqueur into the dry, sterilised bottles, cork, seal and mark. Refrigerate before use.

• CONTAINERS •

Sterilise 1 ℓ bottle.
Makes 950 ml.

CAPE VELVET LIQUEUR

• INGREDIENTS •

397 g tin of condensed milk
410 g tin of evaporated milk
300 ml brandy
10 ml instant coffee powder
10 ml glycerine

• METHOD •

Mix all the ingredients for at least 20 minutes in a food processor or liquidiser.

Pour the liqueur into the dry, sterilised bottles, cork, seal and mark. Refrigerate for a day before use.

• CONTAINERS •

Sterilise 1 ℓ bottle.
Makes 850 ml.

CHERRY CREAM LIQUEUR (1)

• INGREDIENTS •

250 g glazed cherries
2 cloves
2 ml coriander
30 ml white rum
397 g tin of condensed milk
410 g tin of evaporated milk
10 ml glycerine

• METHOD •

Cut the cherries into pieces.

Place the cherries, cloves and coriander in a clean, wide-necked glass bottle with a screw lid. Add the rum, close and mix well. Leave to stand for 12 days. Shake every morning and evening.

Strain the mixture through cheesecloth into a glass bowl. Set aside.

Beat the condensed and evaporated milk and the glycerine for 20 minutes in a mixer. Add the flavoured rum.

Pour the liqueur into the dry, sterilised bottles, cork, seal and mark. Refrigerate for a few days before use.

• CONTAINERS •

Sterilise 1 ℓ bottle.
Makes 1 ℓ.

CHERRY CREAM LIQUEUR (2)

• INGREDIENTS •

250 g fresh black cherries
300 ml brandy
397 ml tin of condensed milk
250 ml fresh cream
15 ml glycerine

• METHOD •

Halve and stone the cherries.

Place the cherries in a wide-necked glass flask with a lid and mash with a potato masher. Add the brandy, mix well and close. Leave to stand for a fortnight in a warm spot. Shake every morning and evening.

Pour the mixture first through a clean sieve and then strain through cheesecloth. Set aside.

Beat the condensed milk, cream and glycerine well in a mixer. Add the flavoured brandy and beat for another 10 minutes.

Pour the liqueur into the dry, sterilised bottles, cork, seal and mark. Refrigerate for a few days before use.

• CONTAINERS •

Sterilise 1 ℓ bottle.
Makes 850 ml.

CHOCOLATE CREAM LIQUEUR (1)

• INGREDIENTS •

75 g Aero peppermint chocolate
397 g tin of condensed milk
250 ml fresh cream
125 ml whisky
125 ml witblits
2 egg yolks
10 ml glycerine
5 ml caramel essence

• METHOD •

Melt the chocolate in a glass bowl over boiling water. Leave to cool slightly.

Mix the remaining ingredients for 15 minutes in a mixer or liquidiser.

Pour the liqueur into the dry, sterilised bottles, cork, seal and mark. Refrigerate for a few days before use.

• CONTAINERS •

Sterilise 1 ℓ bottle.
Makes 900 ml.

Photograph on p 79

CHOCOLATE CREAM LIQUEUR (2)

• INGREDIENTS •

1 big block (200 g) brown and white chocolate
397 g tin of condensed milk
310 g tin of cream
1 egg yolk
10 ml vanilla essence
10 ml glycerine
300 ml brandy

• METHOD •

Break the chocolate into small blocks and melt in a glass bowl over boiling water. Leave to cool slightly.

Mix the remaining ingredients except the brandy for 10 minutes in an electric blender. Add the brandy and beat thoroughly.

Pour the liqueur into the dry, sterilised bottles, cork, seal and mark. Refrigerate for two days before use.

• CONTAINERS •

Sterilise 1 ℓ bottle.
Makes 850 ml.

CHOCOLATE LIQUEUR

• INGREDIENTS •

600 g (750 ml) sugar
750 ml water
750 ml brandy
10 ml vanilla essence
1 ml almond essence
40 ml cocoa, dissolved in 20 ml boiling water

• METHOD •

Place the sugar and water in a heavy-bottomed pot and stir over a low temperature until the sugar has melted. Bring to the boil and boil for 17 minutes. Remove the syrup from the stove and leave to cool. Add the remaining ingredients to the cold syrup and mix well.

Pour the liqueur into the dry, sterilised bottles, cork, seal and mark. Store for a month before use.

• CONTAINERS •

Sterilise 1 ℓ + 250 ml bottles.
Makes 1 ℓ.

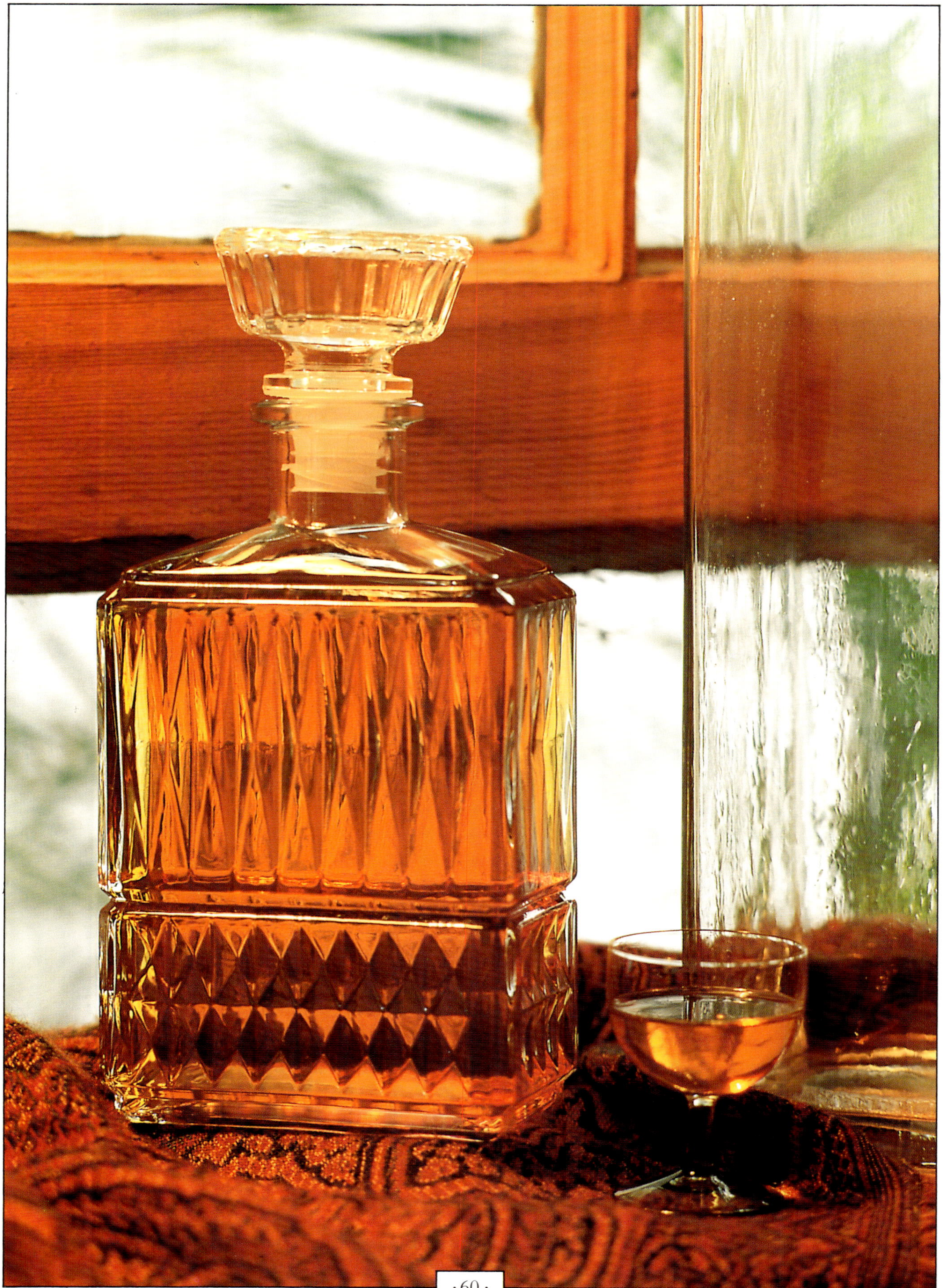

CHOCOLATE VELVET LIQUEUR (1)

• INGREDIENTS •

397 g tin of condensed milk
250 ml fresh cream
4 egg yolks
30 ml chocolate sauce
10 ml instant coffee powder
5 ml vanilla essence
10 ml glycerine
450 ml whisky

• METHOD •

Mix all the ingredients except the whisky for 20 minutes in a mixer or liquidiser. Add the whisky and mix for another minute.
   Pour the liqueur into the dry, sterilised bottles, cork, seal and mark. Refrigerate before use.

• CONTAINERS •

Sterilise 1 ℓ bottle.
Makes 1 ℓ.

CHOCOLATE VELVET LIQUEUR (2)

• INGREDIENTS •

397 g tin of condensed milk
250 ml fresh cream
125 ml whisky
125 ml brandy
2 egg yolks
10 g drinking chocolate
12,5 ml vanilla essence
10 ml glycerine

• METHOD •

Mix all the ingredients for 15 minutes in a mixer or liquidiser.
   Pour the liqueur into the dry, sterilised bottles, cork, seal and mark. Refrigerate before use.

• CONTAINERS •

Sterilise 1 ℓ bottle.
Makes 900 ml.

CITRUS CREAM LIQUEUR

• INGREDIENTS •

2 oranges
2 lemons
12,5 ml naartjie peel, chopped up
1 clove
300 ml schnapps
397 g tin of condensed milk
250 ml fresh cream
15 ml glycerine
yellow food colouing

• METHOD •

Peel the oranges and lemons very thinly with a potato peeler.

Place the orange, lemon and naartjie peel in a glass flask with a lid. Add the clove and schnapps, close and leave to stand for a fortnight in a warm spot. Shake every morning and evening.

Strain the mixture through cheesecloth. Set aside.

Mix the condensed milk, cream, glycerine and a few drops of the dye for 10 minutes in a mixer or liquidiser. Add the flavoured schnapps and mix thoroughly.

Pour the liqueur into the dry, sterilised bottles, cork, seal and mark. Refrigerate before use.

• CONTAINERS •

Sterilise 1 ℓ bottle.
Makes 850 ml.

COCOA COFFEE LIQUEUR

• INGREDIENTS •

750 ml water
600 g (750 ml) brown sugar
25 ml instant coffee powder
20 ml cocoa powder
1 vanilla pod
750 ml cane spirit
125 ml red rum

• METHOD •

Place the water, sugar, coffee powder, cocoa and vanilla pod in a pot. Stir thoroughly, bring to the boil and boil for 17 minutes. Remove the vanilla pod, remove the mixture from the stove and leave to cool. Add the cane and rum and mix well. Leave to stand for a day.

Pour the liqueur into the dry, sterilised bottles, cork, seal and mark. Store for a week before use.

• CONTAINERS •

Sterilise 1 ℓ + 250 ml bottles.
Makes 1,25 ℓ.

COFFEE CREAM LIQUEUR

• INGREDIENTS •

397 g tin of condensed milk
310 g tin of cream
20 ml instant coffee powder
20 ml warm water
10 ml glycerine
5 ml rum essence
250 ml witblits

• METHOD •

Mix the condensed milk and cream. Dissolve the coffee powder in the water and add to the mixture. Beat the glycerine, essence and witblits into the mixture.

Pour the liqueur into the dry, sterilised bottles, cork, seal and mark. Refrigerate for two days before use.

• CONTAINERS •

Sterilise 1 ℓ bottle.
Makes 850 ml.

COFFEE LIQUEUR (1)

• INGREDIENTS •

10 mocha coffee beans, ground
250 ml boiling water
300 g (375 ml) brown sugar
1 ℓ white rum

• METHOD •

Make approximately 250 ml strong coffee with the ground coffee beans and boiling water. Pour the coffee through filter paper, mix immediately with the sugar and stir until the sugar has melted. Leave to cool. Add the rum and mix thoroughly.

Pour the liqueur into the dry, sterilised bottles, cork, seal and mark. Store for a month before use.

• CONTAINERS •

Sterilise 2 x 750 ml bottles.
Makes 1,4 ℓ.

COFFEE LIQUEUR (2)

• INGREDIENTS •

250 ml water
250 g (300 ml) sugar
125 ml strong black
 coffee (real coffee)
190 ml vodka
190 ml cane spirit
100 ml sweet wine
10 ml vanilla
 essence

• METHOD •

Place the water, sugar and coffee in a pot. Mix thoroughly, bring to the boil and boil for 12 minutes. Remove the syrup from the stove and leave to cool. Add the vodka, cane, wine and vanilla.

Pour the liqueur into the dry, sterilised bottles, cork, seal and mark. Store for a month before use.

• CONTAINERS •

Sterilise 1 x 750 ml bottle.
Makes 750 ml.

COFFEE LIQUEUR (3)

• INGREDIENTS •

500 ml warm water
35 ml instant coffee
 powder
600 g (750 ml)
 brown sugar
50 ml red rum
750 ml brandy

• METHOD •

Mix the water and coffee, add the sugar and stir well. Pour into a heavy-bottomed pot, bring to the boil and boil for 15 minutes. Remove from the stove and leave to cool. Add the rum and brandy.

Pour the liqueur into the dry, sterilised bottles, cork, seal and mark. Store for a fortnight before use.

• CONTAINERS •

Sterilise 2 x 750 ml bottles.
Makes 1,4 ℓ.

FIG LEAF CREAM LIQUEUR

• INGREDIENTS •

7 fig leaves
200 ml dry white wine
300 ml cane spirit
397 g tin of condensed milk
310 g tin of cream
10 ml glycerine

• METHOD •

Place the clean fig leaves and wine in a pot. Bring to the boil and boil until the wine is light-green. Remove from the stove and leave to cool.

Add the cane and pour the mixture into a wide-necked glass flask with a lid. Close and leave to stand for six days in a warm spot. Shake regularly.

Strain the mixture through cheesecloth. Set aside.

Mix the condensed milk, cream and glycerine for 15 minutes in a mixer or liquidiser. Add the flavoured alcohol and mix for another five minutes.

Pour the liqueur into the dry, sterilised bottles, cork, seal and mark. Refrigerate for a few day before use.

• CONTAINERS •

Sterilise 1 ℓ bottle.
Makes 900 ml.

GINGER CREAM LIQUEUR

• INGREDIENTS •

25 g fresh ginger root
300 ml witblits
397 g tin of condensed milk
250 ml fresh cream
15 ml glycerine

• METHOD •

Peel and slice the ginger root.

Place the ginger in a glass flask with a screw lid. Add the witblits, close and leave to stand for 12 days in a warm spot. Shake every morning and evening.

Strain the mixture through cheesecloth. Set aside.

Beat the condensed milk, cream and glycerine in a mixer. Add the flavoured witblits and stir thoroughly.

Pour the liqueur into the dry, sterilised bottles, cork, seal and mark. Refrigerate.

• CONTAINERS •

Sterilise 1 ℓ bottle.
Makes 850 ml.

GRANADILLA CREAM LIQUEUR

• INGREDIENTS •

30 granadillas
300 ml vodka
397 g tin of condensed milk
250 ml fresh cream
10 ml glycerine

• METHOD •

Halve the granadillas and remove the pulp.

Place the pulp into a clean glass flask with a lid. Add the vodka, close and leave to stand for about a month in a warm spot. Shake regularly.

Pour the mixture first through a clean sieve and then strain through two layers of cheesecloth. Set aside.

Pour the condensed milk, cream and glycerine into a liquidiser and mix for 10 minutes. Add the flavoured vodka and stir.

Pour the liqueur into the dry, sterilised bottles, cork, seal and mark. Refrigerate for a few days before use.

• CONTAINERS •

Sterilise 1 ℓ bottle.
Makes 850 ml.

GUAVA CREAM LIQUEUR

• INGREDIENTS •

250 g guavas
1 piece of stick cinamon
1 clove
300 ml cane spirit
397 g tin of condensed milk
250 ml fresh cream
10 ml glycerine

• METHOD •

Peel the guavas and cut into pieces.

Place the guava, cinnamon and clove in a clean, dry glass or earthenware container with a lid. Add the cane, close and leave to stand for a fortnight in a warm spot. Shake every morning and evening.

Pour the mixture first through a clean sieve and then strain through cheesecloth. Set aside.

Mix the condensed milk, cream and glycerine well in a mixer or liquidiser. Add the flavoured cane and mix for another 20 minutes.

Pour the liqueur into the dry, sterilised bottles, cork, seal and mark. Refrigerate for three days before use.

• CONTAINERS •

Sterilise 1 l bottle.
Makes 850 ml.

IRISH CREAM LIQUEUR

• INGREDIENTS •

397 g tin of con-
densed milk
300 ml fresh cream
250 ml whisky
15 ml cocoa powder
15 ml warm water
2 drops of almond
essence

• METHOD •

Beat the condensed milk, cream and whisky. Dissolve the cocoa in the water and add the essence. Add to the flavoured whisky and beat for two minutes.

Pour the liqueur into the dry, sterilised bottles, cork, seal and mark. Refrigerate for three days before use.

• CONTAINERS •

Sterilise 1 ℓ bottle.
Makes 850 ml.

Photograph on p 79

LEMON CREAM LIQUEUR

• INGREDIENTS •

2 lemons
2 fresh mint leaves
 (lemon-flavoured)
300 ml cane spirit
397 g tin of con-
densed milk
300 ml evaporated
milk
20 ml glycerine

• METHOD •

Peel the lemons very thinly with a vegetable peeler.

Place the peel and mint in a clean, dry glass flask with a screw lid. Add the cane, close and leave to stand for a fortnight in a warm spot. Shake every morning and evening.

Strain the mixture through cheesecloth. Set aside.

Mix the condensed and evaporated milk and the glycerine thoroughly in a mixer or liquidiser. Add the flavoured cane and mix for 20 minutes.

Pour the liqueur into the dry, sterilised bottles, cork, seal and mark. Refrigerate for four days before use.

• CONTAINERS •

Sterilise 1 ℓ bottle.
Makes 1 ℓ.

LOQUAT CREAM LIQUEUR

• INGREDIENTS •

250 g loquats
2 cm piece of stick cinnamon
300 ml brandy
397 g tin of condensed milk
250 ml fresh cream
10 ml glycerine

• METHOD •

Seed the loquats and cut into pieces.

Place the loquats and cinnamon in a clean, dry flask with a lid. Add the brandy. Close tightly and leave to stand for a month in a warm spot. Shake every day.

Strain the mixture through cheesecloth. Set aside.

Beat the condensed milk, cream and glycerine with a mixer until smooth. Add the flavoured brandy and mix for 20 minutes.

Pour the liqueur into the dry, sterilised bottle, cork, seal and mark. Refrigerate for a day before use.

• CONTAINERS •

Sterilise 1 ℓ bottle.
Makes 850 ml.

MARULA CREAM LIQUEUR

• INGREDIENTS •

500 g marulas
400 ml cane spirit
5 ml fenugreek
397 g tin of condensed milk
250 ml fresh cream
10 ml glycerine

• METHOD •

Peel the marulas.

Place the marulas, cane spirit and fenugreek in a clean, dry glass container with a tight-fitting lid. Leave to stand in a warm spot for three weeks. Shake every morning and evening.

Pour the mixture first through a clean, dry sieve and then strain through two layers of cheesecloth. Set aside.

Mix the condensed milk, cream and glycerine in a liquidiser. Add the marula mixture and mix thoroughly.

Pour the liqueur into the dry, sterilised bottle, cork, seal and mark. Refrigerate for a week before use.

• CONTAINERS •

Sterilise 1 ℓ bottle.
Makes 850 ml.

MULBERRY CREAM LIQUEUR

• INGREDIENTS •

300 g ripe mulberries
pinch of black pepper
1 piece of stick cinnamon
300 ml brandy
397 g tin of condensed milk
250 ml fresh cream
10 ml glycerine

• METHOD •

Remove the stems from the mulberries and place the fruit in a clean glass bowl. Mash the fruit lightly with a potato masher. Sprinkle with the black pepper.

Place the mulberries, together with the cinnamon, in a glass flask with a screw lid. Add the brandy, close and leave to stand in a warm spot for a fortnight. Shake every day.

Strain the mixture through cheesecloth. Set aside.

Mix the condensed milk, cream and glycerine well in a mixer or liquidiser. Add the flavoured brandy and mix for 20 minutes.

Pour the liqueur into the dry, sterilised bottle, cork, seal and mark. Refrigerate for a few days before use.

• CONTAINERS •

Sterilise 1 ℓ bottle.
Makes 850 ml.

MUSKMELON CREAM LIQUEUR

• INGREDIENTS •

500 g muskmelon
2 cardamom seeds
2 slices of fresh ginger root
300 ml witblits
397 g tin of condensed milk
410 g tin of evaporated milk
10 ml glycerine

• METHOD •

Halve, peel and seed the muskmelon. Cut into small pieces.

Place the melon, cardamom and ginger in a wide-necked glass or earthenware container with a lid. Add the witblits, close tightly, shake well and leave to stand for a month in a warm spot. Shake every morning and evening.

Strain the mixture through cheesecloth. Set aside.

Beat the condensed and evaporated milk and the glycerine in a mixer. Add the flavoured witblits and beat for another 20 minutes.

Pour the liqueur into the dry, sterilised bottle, cork, seal and mark. Refrigerate for a few days before use.

• CONTAINERS •

Sterilise 1 ℓ bottle.
Makes 1 ℓ.

NAARTJIE CREAM LIQUEUR

• INGREDIENTS •

1 clove
2 cm piece of stick cinnamon
1 ml ground nutmeg
25 ml grated naartjie peel
300 ml brandy
397 g tin of condensed milk
250 ml fresh cream
10 ml glycerine

• METHOD •

Place the clove, cinnamon, nutmeg and peel in a clean, dry glass or earthenware container with a lid and add the brandy. Close, shake and leave to stand for a month in a warm spot. Shake every morning and evening.

Strain the mixture through cheesecloth. Set aside.

Beat the condensed milk, cream and glycerine well in a mixer. Add the flavoured brandy and beat for another two minutes.

Pour the liqueur into the dry, sterilised bottle, cork, seal and mark. Refrigerate for at least two days before use.

• CONTAINERS •

Sterilise 1 ℓ bottle.
Makes 850 ml.

OATS AND HONEY LIQUEUR

• INGREDIENTS •

50 ml oats
250 ml fresh cream
300 ml whisky
50 ml sherry
50 ml honey

• METHOD •

Mix the oats with a little water and leave to stand overnight.

Place the oats in a small cheesecloth bag and squeeze as much of the water as possible out into a glass bowl. Add the cream and mix very well. Add the whisky, sherry and honey and beat for five minutes in an electric blender. Make sure the honey does not settle at the bottom.

Pour the liqueur into the dry, sterilised bottle, cork, seal and mark. Refrigerate for about five days, leave to stand for about an hour at room temperature and shake well before use.

• CONTAINERS •

Sterilise 1 x 750 ml bottle.
Makes 750 ml.

ORANGE, BANANA, STRAWBERRY OR PINEAPPLE LIQUEUR

• INGREDIENTS •

397 g tin of con-
densed milk
250 ml fresh cream
375 ml brandy
45 ml orange,
banana, strawberry
or pineapple essence
10 ml glycerine
3 ml yellow or red
food colouring

• METHOD •

Mix all the ingredients in a mixer or liquidiser.
 Pour the liqueur into the dry, sterilised bottle, cork, seal and mark. Refrigerate before use.

• CONTAINERS •

Sterilise 1 ℓ bottle.
Makes 950 ml.

ORANGE CREAM LIQUEUR

• INGREDIENTS •

2 sweet oranges
1 ml ground
 cinnamon
1 clove
300 ml brandy
397 g tin of con-
densed milk
410 g tin of evaporated
 milk
15 ml glycerine
yellow food colouring

• METHOD •

Peel the oranges very thinly with a vegetable peeler. Shred finely. Remove the pith from the flesh and cut into pieces.
 Place the peel, flesh, cinnamon and clove in a big, dry glass flask with a lid. Add the brandy, close and leave to stand for a fortnight. Shake regularly.
 Pour the mixture first through a clean sieve and then strain through cheesecloth into a glass bowl. Set aside.
 Beat the condensed and evaporated milk, the glycerine and the dye for at least 10 minutes in a mixer. Add the flavoured brandy and mix well.
 Pour the liqueur into the dry, sterilised bottle, cork, seal and mark. Refrigerate for a day before use.

• CONTAINERS •

Sterilise 1 ℓ bottle.
Makes 1 ℓ.

PAPINO CREAM LIQUEUR

• INGREDIENTS •

250 g fresh papino
½ vanilla pod
300 ml white rum
397 g tin of con‐
 densed milk
250 ml fresh cream
10 ml glycerine

• METHOD •

Peel, halve and seed the papino. Cut into quarters. Break the vanilla pod into pieces.

Place the papino and vanilla in a glass flask with a lid. Add the rum, close and leave to stand for 10 days in a warm spot. Shake every morning and evening.

Strain the mixture through cheesecloth into a glass bowl. Set aside.

Mix the condensed milk, cream and glycerine for 10 minutes in a mixer, liquidiser or food processor. Add the flavoured rum and mix for 10 minutes.

Pour the liqueur into the dry, sterilised bottle, cork, seal and mark. Refrigerate for two days before use.

• CONTAINERS •

Sterilise 1 ℓ bottle.
Makes 850 ml.

PEACH CREAM LIQUEUR (1)

• INGREDIENTS •

300 ml peach nectar
250 ml Jerepigo
300 ml gin
1 ml ground nutmeg
397 g tin of con‐
 densed milk
250 ml fresh cream
10 ml glycerine

• METHOD •

Mix all the ingredients for 10 minutes in a food processor or liquidiser.

Pour the liqueur into the dry, sterilised bottles, cork, seal and mark. Refrigerate before use.

• CONTAINERS •

Sterilise 2 x 750 ml bottles.
Makes 1,4 ℓ.

PEACH CREAM LIQUEUR (2)

• INGREDIENTS •

250 g clingstone peaches
1 ml ground nutmeg
300 ml brandy
397 g tin of condensed milk
250 ml fresh cream
10 ml glycerine
yellow food colouring

• METHOD •

Halve and stone the peaches, retaining the stones. Slice the peaches. Crack the stones, remove the kernels and pull off the skins.

Place the peaches, kernels and nutmeg in a clean, dry glass flask with a screw lid. Add the brandy, close and leave to stand for a fortnight. Shake every morning and evening.

Strain the mixture through cheesecloth and squeeze out as much as possible of the flavoured brandy. Set aside.

Mix the condensed milk, cream and glycerine for 10 minutes in a mixer or liquidiser. Add just enough dye to make the mixture light-yellow. Add the flavoured brandy and mix for another 10 minutes.

Pour the liqueur into the dry, sterilised bottle, cork, seal and mark. Refrigerate for at least two days before use.

• CONTAINERS •

Sterilise 1 ℓ bottle.
Makes 850 ml.

PEPPERMINT CREAM LIQUEUR

• INGREDIENTS •

300 ml cane spirit
37,5 ml white rum
peppermint oil
397 g tin of condensed milk
250 ml fresh cream
15 ml glycerine
green food colouring

• METHOD •

Mix the cane, rum and a few drops of the peppermint oil. Mix the condensed milk, cream and glycerine for 15 minutes in a liquidiser. Add the flavoured alcohol and colouring (enough for an attractive green colour) and stir well.

Pour the liqueur into the dry, sterilised bottle, cork, seal and mark. Refrigerate for 12 hours before use.

• CONTAINERS •

Sterilise 1 ℓ bottle.
Makes 850 ml.

PEPPERMINT LIQUEUR

• INGREDIENTS •

400 g (500 ml) sugar
600 ml water
750 ml brandy
50 ml gin
peppermint oil
green food colouring

• METHOD •

Mix the sugar and water in a heavy-bottomed pot, bring to the boil and boil for 17 minutes. Remove the syrup from the stove and leave to cool. Add the brandy, gin, a few drops of the peppermint oil and colouring (enough for an attractive green colour) to the syrup and stir well.

Pour the liqueur into the dry, sterilised bottles, cork, seal and mark. Store for 3 weeks before use.

• CONTAINERS •

Sterilise 1 ℓ + 250 ml bottles.
Makes 1,2 ℓ.

PINEAPPLE CREAM LIQUEUR

• INGREDIENTS •

250 ml pineapple (½ pineapple)
300 ml brandy
397 g tin of condensed milk
250 ml fresh cream
10 ml glycerine

• METHOD •

Peel the pineapple, retaining the peel. Remove the core and eyes. Cut into pieces.

Place the peel and flesh in a wide-necked glass flask with a screw lid. Add the brandy, close and leave to stand for a month in a warm spot. Shake every morning and evening.

Pour the mixture first through a clean sieve and then strain through cheesecloth. Set aside.

Mix the condensed milk, cream and glycerine for 15 minutes in a mixer or liquidiser. Add the flavoured brandy and mix for another five minutes.

Pour the liqueur into the dry, sterilised bottle, cork, seal and mark. Refrigerate for two days before use.

• CONTAINERS •

Sterilise 1 ℓ bottle.
Makes 850 ml.

POMEGRANATE CREAM LIQUEUR

• INGREDIENTS •

250 g pomegranate pips
1 sprig of fresh fennel
50 ml red Jerepigo
300 ml vodka
397 g tin of condensed milk
250 ml fresh cream
10 ml glycerine

• METHOD •

Place the pips and fennel in a glass or earthenware container with a lid. Add the jerepigo and vodka, close tightly and leave to stand for a fortnight in a warm spot. Shake every morning and evening.

Pour the mixture first through a clean sieve and then strain through cheesecloth. Set aside.

Beat the condensed milk, cream and glycerine well in a mixer. Add the flavoured brandy and beat for another 10 minutes.

Pour the liqueur into the dry, sterilised bottle, cork, seal and mark. Refrigerate for a few days before use.

• CONTAINERS •

Sterilise 1 ℓ bottle.
Makes 900 ml.

PLUM CREAM LIQUEUR

• INGREDIENTS •

250 g fresh plums
300 ml gin
50 ml red rum
397 g tin of condensed milk
410 g tin of evaporated milk
10 ml glycerine

• METHOD •

Halve, stone and cut the plums into pieces.

Place the plums in a clean glass or earthenware container with a lid. Add the gin and rum, mix thoroughly and close. Leave to stand for a month in a warm spot. Shake every morning and evening.

Strain the mixture through two layers of cheesecloth. Set aside.

Mix the condensed and evaporated milk and the glycerine in a liquidiser until smooth and creamy. Add the flavoured gin and red rum and mix for another 20 minutes.

Pour the liqueur into the dry, sterilised bottle, cork, seal and mark. Refrigerate for a few days before use.

• CONTAINERS •

Sterilise 1 ℓ bottle.
Makes 1 ℓ.

ROSE PETAL CREAM LIQUEUR

• INGREDIENTS •

10 red roses
300 ml gin
397 g tin of condensed milk
410 g tin of evaporated milk
10 ml glycerine
2 ml rosewater

• METHOD •

Remove the clean petals from the roses. Place in a clean glass flask with a lid. Add the gin, close tightly and leave to stand in a warm spot for six weeks. Shake regularly.

Strain the mixture through cheesecloth. Set aside.

Mix the condensed and evaporated milk, the glycerine and the rosewater well in a liquidiser. Add the flavoured gin and mix for another 20 minutes.

Pour the liqueur into the dry, sterilised bottle, cork, seal and mark. Refrigerate for three days before use.

• CONTAINERS •

Sterilise 1 ℓ bottle.
Makes 1 ℓ.

STRAWBERRY CREAM LIQUEUR

• INGREDIENTS •

250 g fresh strawberries
1 ml black pepper
300 ml witblits
397 g tin of condensed milk
410 g tin of evaporated milk
or
250 ml fresh cream
15 ml glycerine

• METHOD •

Remove the stems and leaves from the strawberries. Halve and sprinkle the strawberries with black pepper.

Place in a wide-necked glass flask with a lid. Add the witblits, close and leave to stand for 20 days in a warm spot. Shake every morning and evening.

Pour the mixture first through a clean sieve and then strain through cheesecloth. Set aside.

Beat the condensed milk, evaporated milk or cream and glycerine for 10 minutes in a mixer. Add the flavoured witblits and beat for another 10 minutes.

Pour the liqueur into the dry, sterilised bottle, cork, seal and mark. Refrigerate for two days before use.

• CONTAINERS •

Sterilise 1 ℓ bottle.
Makes 1 ℓ.

SWEET MELON CREAM LIQUEUR

• INGREDIENTS •

500 g sweet melon
1 ml ground ginger
3 cardamom seeds
300 ml white rum
397 g tin of condensed milk
410 g tin of evaporated milk
10 ml glycerine

• METHOD •

Halve, peel and seed the sweet melon. Cut into pieces.

Place the melon, ginger and cardamom in a glass container with a lid. Add the rum, close and leave to stand for three weeks in a warm spot. Shake every morning and evening.

Strain the mixture through cheesecloth. Set aside.

Mix the condensed and evaporated milk and the glycerine for 10 minutes in a mixer or liquidiser. Add the flavoured rum and mix for another 10 minutes.

Pour the liqueur into the dry, sterilised bottle, cork, seal and mark. Refrigerate for two days before use.

• CONTAINERS •

Sterilise 1 ℓ bottle.
Makes 1 ℓ.

TROPICAL CREAM LIQUEUR

• INGREDIENTS •

150 g fresh pineapple
100 g fresh guava
100 g papino
2 cardamom seeds
5 ml allspice
300 ml gin
15 ml rum
15 ml brandy
397 g tin of condensed milk
410 g tin of evaporated milk
10 ml glycerine

• METHOD •

Peel the fruit. Remove the core and eyes from the pineapple. Seed the guava and papino. Cut the fruit into small pieces, place in a liquidiser and liquidise until pulped but not pureed.

Place the pulp, cardamom and allspice in a big glass flask with a screw lid. Add the gin, rum and brandy. Close, shake and leave to stand for two months in a warm spot. Shake every morning and evening.

Strain the mixture through cheesecloth into a glass bowl. Set aside.

Beat the condensed and evaporated milk and the glycerine in a mixer until smooth. Add the flavoured alcohol and mix for 20 minutes.

Pour the liqueur into the dry, sterilised bottle, cork, seal and mark. Refrigerate for at least two days before use.

• CONTAINERS •

Sterilise 1 ℓ bottle
Makes 1 ℓ.

VANILLA CREAM LIQUEUR

• INGREDIENTS •

1 vanilla pod
300 ml brandy
397 g tin of con-
   densed milk
250 ml fresh cream
10 ml glycerine

• METHOD •

Cut the vanilla pod lengthwise and break into small pieces.
   Place the vanilla in a clean glass flask with a screw lid. Add the brandy, close, shake well and leave to stand for a month in a warm spot. Shake every morning and evening.
   Strain the mixture through cheesecloth. Set aside.
   Mix the condensed milk, cream and glycerine for 10 minutes in a liquidiser. Add the flavoured brandy and mix for another 10 minutes.
   Pour the liqueur into the dry, sterilised bottle, cork, seal and mark. Refrigerate for a few days before use.

• CONTAINERS •

Sterilise 1 ℓ bottle.
Makes 850 ml.

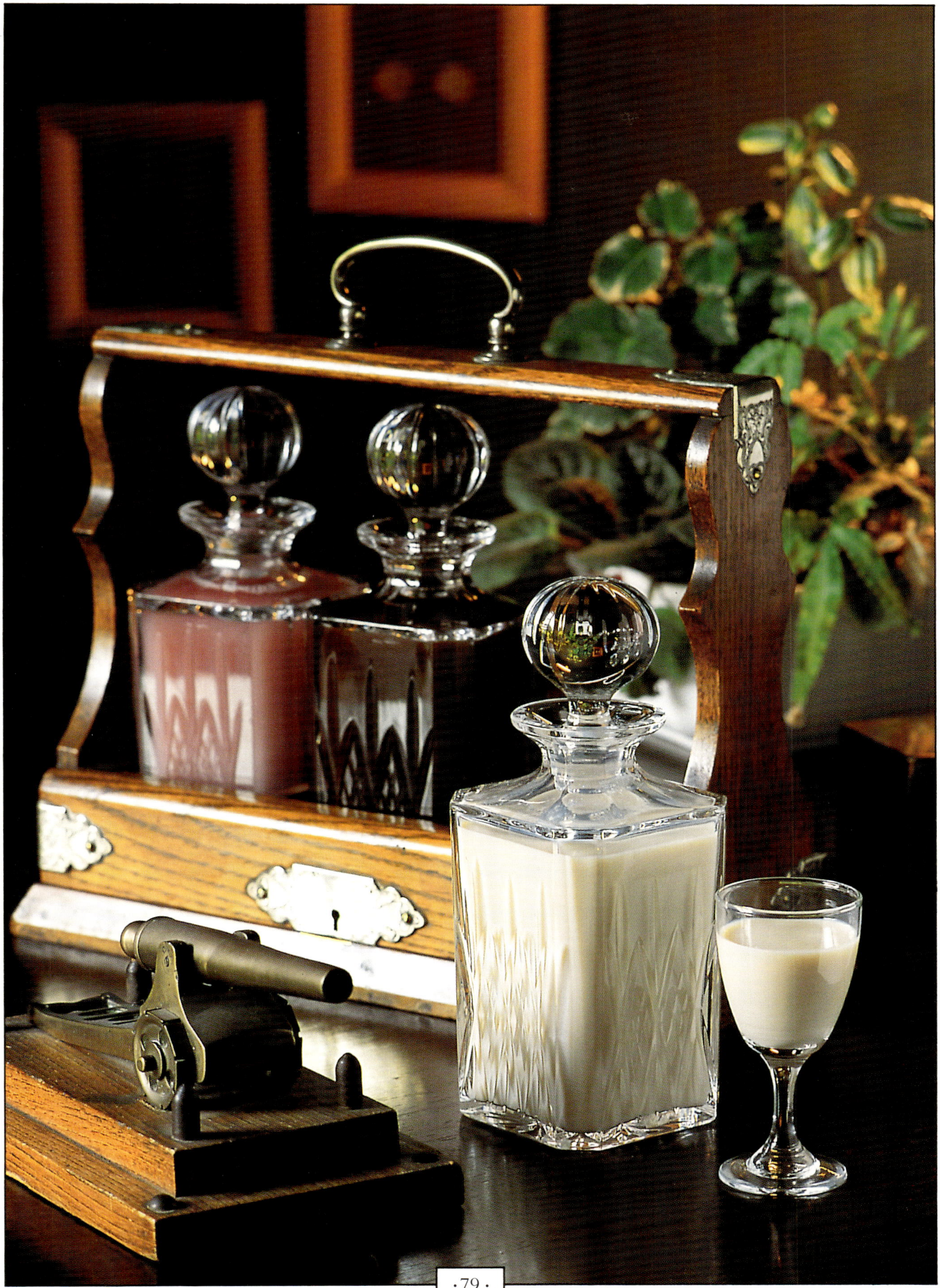

Index

Fruit liqueur with an alcohol and sugar base

Angelica 18
Aniseed 19
Apple and fennel 19
Apple 20
Apricot (1) 20
Apricot (2) 21
Banana 21
Blackberry (1) 22
Blackberry (2) 22
Blueberry 23
Carnation 23
Cherry 24
Cherry stone 24
Citrus 25
Coffee bean 25
Coffee 26
Elder 26
Fig leaf 27
Granadilla 27
Grapefruit 28
Green walnut 28
Guava 30
Hyssop 30
Kummel 31
Lemon 31
Litchi 32
Loquat 32
Love 33
Mango 33
Marula 34
Mulberry 34
Muskmelon (1) 35
Muskmelon (2) 35
Naartjie 36
Orange blossom 36
Orange (1) 37
Orange (2) 37
Orange (3) 38
Papino 38
Peach leaf 39
Peach (1) 39
Peach (2) 40
Peach stone 40
Pear 41
Peel 41
Pineapple (1) 43

Pineapple (2) 43
Pineapple (3) 44
Plum (1) 44
Plum (2) 45
Pomgrenate 45
Red rose petal 46
Rhubarb 46
Seville 47
Strawberry (1) 47
Strawberry (2) 48
Sweet melon 48
Tropical 49
Van der Hum 49
Vanilla 50
Verbena 50
Violet 51

Fruit cream and instant liqueur

Advocaat (1) 53
Advocaat (2) 54
Aniseed cream 54
Apricot cream 55
Banana cream 55
Blackberry cream 56
Blueberry cream 56
Cape velvet 57
Cherry cream (1) 57
Cherry cream (2) 58
Chocolate cream (1) 58
Chocolate cream (2) 59
Chocolate 59
Chocolate velvet (1) 61
Chocolate velvet (2) 61
Citrus cream 62
Cocoa coffee 62
Coffee cream 63
Coffee (1) 63
Coffee (2) 64
Coffee (3) 64
Fig leaf cream 65
Ginger cream 65
Granadilla cream 66
Guava cream 66
Irish cream 67
Lemon cream 67
Loquat cream 68
Marula cream 68
Mulberry cream 69

Muskmelon cream 69
Naartjie cream 70
Oats and honey 70
Orange, banana, strawberry or pineapple 71
Orange cream 71
Papino cream 72
Peach cream (1) 72
Peach cream (2) 73
Peppermint cream 73
Peppermint 74
Pineapple cream 74
Plum cream 75
Pomegranate cream 75
Rose petal cream 76
Strawberry cream 76
Sweet melon cream 77
Tropical cream 77
Vanilla cream 78